The Beagle

Catherine Sutton

KW-263-066

John Bartholomew & Son Limited
Edinburgh and London

The Publisher wishes to thank The Kennel Club and The American Kennel Club for permission to reproduce the breed standards.

First published in Great Britain 1977 *by*
JOHN BARTHOLOMEW & SON LIMITED
12 Duncan Street, Edinburgh EH9 1TA
And at 216 High Street, Bromley BR1 1PW

ISBN 0 7028 1045 2

1st edition

Prepared for the Publisher by Youé & Spooner Ltd.
Colour illustrations by Tony Spalding; airbrush drawings by Malcolm Ward

Printed in Great Britain by John Bartholomew & Son Limited

Contents

Cover illustration:
The merry Beagle makes an attractive pet, even while not of show standard

Preface

Merry, active, smart as paint, it is easy to see why the Beagle is so immensely popular on both sides of the Atlantic. This book is written by one of the greatest Beagle experts for all those who love the breed and all those who are thinking of buying one. A breed with so long a history as a hunting dog has adapted in the last few decades with remarkable success to being a pet and companion animal enjoying life in both urban and country settings. This book tells you all you need to know to get the best out of your relationship with your dog. We hope it will lead you on to even further pleasures such as breeding and showing your dog. The chapter on hunting may tempt many Beagle owners to try a day's sport which can only give them a better insight and greater admiration for so versatile a little hound.

Wendy Boorer
Consultant Editor

Breed history

The Beagle is one of the oldest of all the pure hound breeds and can truthfully be claimed to be as essentially British as any other existing canine. No one who has ever had the pleasure of knowing a Beagle could possibly deny that this little hound is one of the most charming in the Hound Group. It has great character. It is sturdy with tremendous stamina and activity and yet, in the home, is a very lovable companion, a much desired friend and generally a grand little person.

Today in Great Britain there are about eighty packs of hunting Beagles up and down the country. These hounds have originated from the hunting hounds of the past and it is in these pack hounds that our show hounds have their forefathers.

The Beagle's history is rather vague, and many and varied are the theories put forward as to when it first arrived and who was responsible for it. Sufficient to say that in Britain, at the end of 1975, we had 1,875 Beagles registered at the Kennel Club as show hounds apart from the registered Hunting Packs. This is the lowest total for many years and considerably less than when they reached their peak in 1969 with 3,979 Beagles registered. Serious breeders welcome this downward trend as, when a breed becomes too popular, haphazard breeding by every Tom, Dick and Harry takes place in the hope of turning over a quick dime. Conscientious and dedicated breeders are much more interested in quality rather than quantity.

The Beagle is mentioned many times in very early literature but the first traceable mention as 'Beagles' was in 1475 in *The Squire of Low Degree:*

> *'With theyr beagles in that place*
> *and seven score raches at his rechase.'*

Some authorities feel that the breed was mentioned before this, but this does not seem to have been confirmed, although if one cares to study the early murals and pictures, long before 1475, the Beagle certainly seemed to be in existence. It appears as a low to ground hound with its ears hanging forward towards its mouth. What they were named in these days is not really certain, but I am perfectly sure that some of the good old hunting men of days gone by would have several choice names for them on occasions, just as they have today!

It is said that the name 'Beagle' goes back to the time of the invasion of England in 1066 when the French tongue was brought to Britain by the invading Normans. The word 'beagle' could, therefore, perhaps be a derivation from the French word *'Bégueule',* (from *béer* meaning to 'to gape' and from *gueule* meaning 'throat'). On the other hand some prefer to think that the word went back to the Old English word *'begle'* meaning small, or to the Celtic *'beag'* which again means small.

Beagles are natural hunters and given the opportunity, plus a bit of encouragement, they soon adapt themselves to this sport. In the far off days when man decided so wisely to befriend the canine race he quickly taught them to hunt. This, of course, was a most sensible thing to do as so often it meant that he was assured of a supper rather than having to go without.

Gervase Markham, writing in *Country Contentments* published in 1631, declares that in his opinion all the dogs used by sportsmen in pursuit of their quarry were each and all of them 'the same kinde of creatures, namely hounds'. The white hound, or the white hound with black spots, seemed to be favoured by Mr. Markham and it is felt by many that in those far off days our present Fox Terriers had very close connections with these hounds. It is not just the colour alone that gives this impression but the formation of the head and the length of ears.

From the works of the Ancient Greek author Xenophon, born about 433 BC, it is quite clear that he refers to small hounds that were used to hunt the hare on foot. It can reasonably be assumed that they were in fact beagles or very close to them. Xenophon's detailed descriptions of the hunt were most realistic and some of his sayings are still used today. For instance, he talked of 'babblers' and 'mutes' and disliked their inclusion in any pack just as our Masters of Hounds discard them today. A 'babbler' is a hound that gives tongue for no reason at all and in reverse a 'mute' is a hound that is following a scent without giving tongue and therefore keeping the discovery of the scent to himself. Both are quite useless in a good hunting pack.

The Book of Field Sports by Dame Juliana Berners is the earliest work actually printed in the English language in which are given and listed definite breeds of dogs that were then in existence. Dame Juliana, who was said to be the Prioress of Sopwell Nunnery in Hertfordshire, England, was considered to

Points of the Beagle

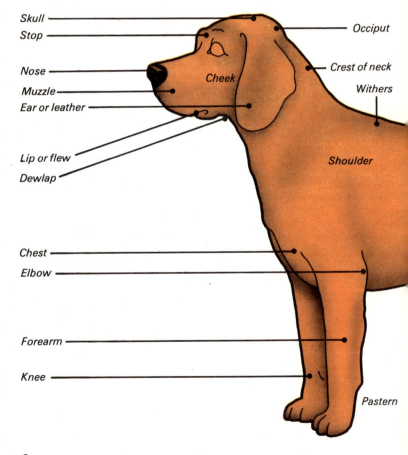

Skull

Stop

Nose

Muzzle

Ear or leather

Lip or flew

Dewlap

Chest

Elbow

Forearm

Knee

Occiput

Crest of neck

Withers

Cheek

Shoulder

Pastern

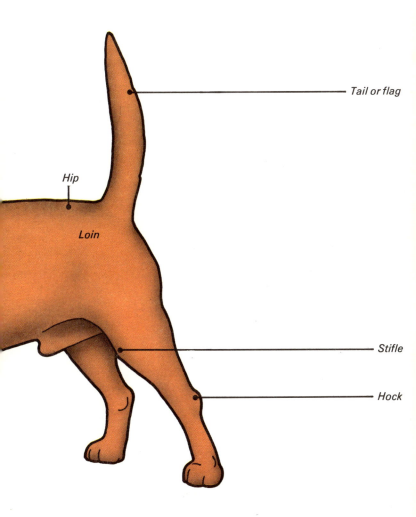

Tail or flag

Hip

Loin

Stifle

Hock

be a very great authority on hunting during her lifetime which was the beginning of the fifteenth century. The breeds she listed in her *Book of Field Sports* were as follows: 'Thyse ben the names of houndes, fyrste there is a Grehoun, a Bastard, a Mengrell, a Mastif, a Lemor, a Spanyel, Raches, Kennettys, Teroures, Butchers Houndes, Dunghyll dogges, Tryndeltaylles, and Pryckeryd currys, and smalle ladyes poppees that bere awaye the flees.'

Today the English Kennel Club lists well over one hundred breeds. From Dame Juliana's list one can recognise many of the breeds of dog that are with us today.

It is perhaps slightly difficult to recognise the Beagle from Dame Juliana's list but the word Kennettys was defined in Wright and Thomas's *Dictionary of Obsolete and Provisional English* as being a small hound and this could apply to our Beagle.

Edward the Confessor was known to hunt Kennettys in the eleventh century and Chaucer in his well known *Canterbury Tales* refers to the 'smalle hounds'. It is thought that these 'smalle hounds' included the Beagle, the Basset and the Dachshund of that day. The larger hounds perhaps came into the category of 'Raches', a word that was used very frequently in early hunting literature, and it seems likely that this would refer to our present day Harrier.

In 1576, Dr. John Caius, physician to Queen Elizabeth, published a work that had been originally written in Latin and translated by Abraham Fleming and entitled *of Englishe Dogges.* This was the first work ever which was solely confined to the various different breeds or types of dog and the manner of hunting them. Dr. Caius maintained that 'All English Dogges be eyther of –

      (a) A gentle kind, serving the game.
      (b) A homely kind, apt for sundry necessary uses.
      (c) A currish kind, meet for many toyes.'

The author divided the first of these three types into two quite different and definite categories. The *Venatici* used for the purpose of hunting beasts and the *Aucupatorii* in the pursuit of fowl. It seems quite obvious that our Beagles came in the first class and that the gundogs were included in the second class.

As Beagle lovers we are proud to think that the Beagle has been a very firm favourite in many Royal Households. Queen

Elizabeth I had a pack of pocket Beagles that are reputed to have measured not more than 10in. (25cm.) and they were often referred to as singing Beagles. It is said that some of them were so small that they could get inside a lady's glove or gauntlet. The fashion in gloves has certainly changed from Queen Elizabeth's time, and so has the fashion in Beagles, as I doubt if there are more than just a handful of typical Beagles of under 10in. (25cm.) alive today.

Around the middle of the eighteenth century, a Colonel Hardy had a collection of very small Beagles that were always carried to and from the hunt in a large pair of panniers slung across a horse. Although small they were tough little characters and very capable of hunting the hare and making a kill. Some writers have described it as 'teasing her to death'.

The last known pack of small Beagles was owned by a Mr. James Crane of Dorchester, and Idstone (Rev. Thomas Pearce) referred to this pack in his book *The Dog* published in 1872, as probably the best pack of Beagles ever bred. Idstone goes on to say that at his urgent request Mr. Crane exhibited them once or twice with complete success, winning everywhere. Idstone believes that Mr. Crane originally took to the Beagles to rid himself of the rabbits which had become quite an annoyance on his ground. I quote from Idstone's book: 'A very few years ago "Giant" was the dwarf of the pack; now he is drafted as too large, whilst as to formation they are equal to the Poltimore or Belvoir Hounds. They go through the performance of a regular pack, with supreme gravity (as Foxhounds would think, if they do think, like a set of puppets). It has a serio-comic appearance to see Mr. Crane start from his Lilliputian kennel, with its dog doll's house furniture of troughs and beds, followed by a pack of Hounds not so large as rabbits, of the recognised colours and markings, and with all the importance of full sized Staghounds!' It is little wonder that Idstone thought it a great treat to have a day's hunting with these beautiful miniatures.

The standard height of the whole of Mr. Crane's pack was about 9in. (23cm.) and, due to their wonderful hindquarters and general frame and development, they could account for a rabbit in about five minutes. There was a great variety of colour in this pack and it added to their beauty and, in Idstone's opinion, it proved them identical in family with the Southern Hound or Harrier.

This beautiful little pack had a very sad ending and I quote from Stonehenge (J.H. Walsh) 1886: 'Many of his mothers do not rear their offspring, and distemper carries them off in troops.' That awful scourge distemper played havoc with his grand little hounds and in 1894, Mr. Crane died, many thought of a broken heart.

Going back to the Royal owners of our breed, we find that King James I (1566-1625) was a very ardent and enthusiastic supporter of the hunting field and enjoyed his hare-hunting, not on foot, but on horseback. It is said that this great character often referred to his Queen as his 'deare littel beagle'.

Charles II (1630-1685) was yet another monarch who loved to hunt his beagles, and his hunting ground was Newmarket Heath. William III (William of Orange, 1689-1702) followed on with many exciting and entertaining hunts by his game little Beagles. King George IV hunted a pack in the Brighton area and later Prince Albert, Consort to Queen Victoria, had a very excellent pack that hunted hare and rabbit in Windsor Forest. The Fifth Earl of Bedford hunted a good pack in the middle of the seventeenth century. Gladys Scott Thomson, in her book *Life in a Noble Household,* confirms this when she quotes a letter from the Earl to his son in which he stated: 'I shall not bring my beagles, only my hawks.' The keeping of hawks for pastime and pleasure was a very noble recreation in those days.

Sporting Anecdotes (1807) refers to the Beagle and states that the small dogs were capable of tiring the strongest hunters and returning quite fresh to their kennels. Although Beagles are not normally hunted on horseback today, they are very capable of tiring even the fittest follower of hounds, and no one would dispute that their tremendous stamina and energy is very much part of their make-up.

To those of you who have never had the opportunity to hunt with Beagles, to watch them work or to listen to their music, it would be difficult for me even to attempt to tell you how very much you have missed. Not only is there the excitement but also the joy of listening to their little tongues, the soft yet melodious music, and the glories of the countryside with its own special magic.

I quote from the *Sportsman's Cabinet* of 1803: 'They are the smallest of the hound race used in this country, are exquisite in their scent of the hare, and indefatigably vigilant in their pursuit of her. This slow kind of hunting was admirably adapted to age and feminine gender. It could be enjoyed by the ladies of the greatest timidity, as well as gentlemen labouring under infirmity, to both of whom it was a consolation that if they were occasionally a little way behind, there was barely a possibility of their being thrown out. A pack of this description was perfectly accommodating to the neighbouring rustics – the major part of those not being possessed of horses found it a matter of no great difficulty to be up well with them on foot.'

In the pack hounds of today, as in the past, the type varies according to the country hunted. Somerville wrote in the eighteenth century: 'A different hound for every chase: Select with Judgement.' These last three words are surely applicable today to breeders of our show stock as well as to the Masters and their Huntsmen. Wise words indeed and they should apply not only to the selection of stud dog and brood bitch. (See the chapter on Breeding.)

By the nineteenth century type was stabilising itself and was much more typical of our present day Kennel Club Standard. Stonehenge in his *Manual of British Sports* (1861) gave the varieties of the breed as follows: 'First, the medium Beagle which may be either heavy and Southern-like, or light and Northern-like; second, the dwarf or lap dog Beagle; third the Fox Beagle; and fourth the rough or Terrier Beagle.' Stonehenge insisted that the breed should be free from jealousy (he meant the hounds), and that they should co-operate to the full and have great patience in the hunting field. He wanted Lilliputian dimensions and, of course, a good nose. In the *Field* of 1855 this great sportsman described the Beagle as a model of a foxhound, a 'pocket lexicon'.

Although very rarely seen today, rough-coated Beagles were found in Wales. It is a great pity that this variety has disappeared and perhaps the last time a group of these was seen in public was at Reigate, England, early this century when the Telescombe were exhibited by Mr. Gorham.

Finally we have the Kerry Beagle, quite a different hound from the general idea of what a Beagle should look like. This is an upstanding, rather lightly built black/tan hound and in many ways is akin to the Bloodhound. The breed has been known in Ireland for more than 200 years and the Ryan family of Scarteen claimed to have owned them since 1735. They were not seen in England until the early years of this century and I doubt very much if any now remain.

The Beagle Club of England was formed in 1890 and in the following year the Association of Masters of Harriers and Beagles was established. The object of both bodies was to further the best interests of the Beagle. The Association's Members are confined to those who keep or have kept registered packs which regularly hunt the hare. The Beagle Club, on the other hand, opens its doors to any true lover of the Beagle. The objects of this Club were originally published in 1899 and they are still the same today and as follows:

'It keeps wide open its doors and welcomes alike to the fold the Master of Beagles who wishes to maintain or form his Pack on ancient lines; the shooting man who keeps a few couples for driving out the rabbits, or putting up the pheasant; the drag hunter who gets an afternoon's healthy exercise with the pleasure of seeing hounds work and hearing hound music; the exhibitor who finds pleasure in breeding for perfection, so far as looks go, and performs most useful work by making the beauty of the breed more generally known; the lady who finds the Beagle the most intelligent and interesting of pets; last, but certainly not the least, the old sportsman whose sporting days are over, who has a keen remembrance of what has been and joins in, while his recollections and experiences are of inestimable value to a younger generation. All these are now united in the same effort.'

The Beagle Club has now been joined by several other specialist clubs all sharing the same common interest – the Beagle.

The English Kennel Club was formed in 1873 and it was not until that date that shows were held regularly and under the Kennel Club's Rules and Regulations.

In 1927 a total of seven Beagles were registered at the Kennel Club and two Championship Shows were allocated Challenge Certificates at which the entry in the Open classes averaged about two. Progress was made rather slowly until 1958 when 635 Beagles were registered. In 1945, because of the war, the registrations fell back to one Beagle only. In 1951 just over 100 were registered and registrations continued to increase until in 1969 the peak was reached with 3,979 Beagles registered.

The first Champion ever made up in Britain was a bitch in 1926 called the Belton Scornful and she was owned by Mrs. Beaumont and bred by Mr. Roberts on 18 July 1920. She was by The Stock Place Schoolboy ex Montgomeryshire Madcap. The first dog to be made a Champion was Mrs. Beaumont's Bilton Pedlar and this was in 1927. Bred by Mrs. Beaumont he was born on 9 June 1923, by Bilton Plunderer ex the aforementioned Champion bitch.

At the time of writing, August 1976, 120 bitches and ninety-five males have gained their crowns.

Today Beagles have classes at most of the large Open Shows and certainly at all the General Championship Shows, plus Breed Club Specialist Championship Shows. At our major Championship Shows and Club Ch. Shows one can expect anything from 150 to 200 Beagles to be entered.

All through the ages our little hound has played his part – be it in the hunting field, on the show bench or just by the fireside as a loyal and happy companion. We, who are privileged to know them and, I hope, to understand them, can ask no more than that they continue to receive all the love and care that they richly deserve, plus the fun and the excitement of the chase that they have known for so long, right back through the distant ages.

The breed standard

The Standard of the Beagle as laid down by the Kennel Club is a very simple one, free from frills, and one that should be easily understood and interpreted by most people and certainly by all judges of the breed. The Standard is the guideline for all interested in breeding and must certainly be the bible for those adjudicating.

Of course, there will always be slightly different interpretations of the Standard by individuals, but these should not vary to any great degree, so that the dogs themselves should all present a fairly level picture both in type and conformation. Tragically, for the breed, this is not always so. This could stem from the irresponsible, who do not even bother to read the Standard before judging or study it in great detail before breeding.

Let us look at the Standard which was revised by the Kennel Club, with the co-operation of the Breed Clubs, in April 1973.

The British Breed Standard

Characteristics *A merry hound whose essential function is to hunt, primarily hare, by following a scent. Bold with great activity, stamina and determination. Alert, intelligent and of even temperament.*

General Appearance *A sturdy and compactly built hound, conveying the impression of quality without coarseness.*

Head and Skull *Head fair length, powerful in the dog without being coarse, but finer in the bitch; free from frown and excessive wrinkle. Skull slightly domed, moderately wide, with indication of peak. Stop well defined and dividing length between occiput and tip of nose as equally as possible. Muzzle not snipy, lips reasonably well flewed. Nose broad and nostrils well expanded; preferably black, but less pigmentation permissible in the lighter coloured hounds.*

Eyes *Dark brown or hazel, fairly large, not deep set or bulgy, set well apart and with a mild appealing expression.*

(NB Although this is very explicit, it is surprising how many black eyed Beagles we do see and, of course, the mild appealing expression is lost.)

Ears *Long with round tip, reaching nearly to end of nose when drawn out. Set on low, fine in texture and hanging gracefully close to cheek.*

Mouth *Teeth strongly developed. Upper incisors just overlapping and touching outer surface of lower incisors to form a scissor bite.*

Neck *Sufficiently long to enable hound to come down easily to scent, slightly arched and showing a little dewlap.*

Forequarters *Shoulder clean and sloping. Forelegs straight and upright, well under the hound, of good substance, strong, hard and round in bone. Not tapering off to feet. Pasterns short. Elbows firm, turning neither in nor out. Height to elbow about half the hound's height to withers.*

Skeleton of the Beagle

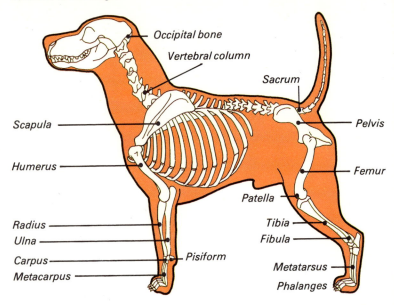

Occipital bone
Vertebral column
Sacrum
Scapula
Pelvis
Humerus
Femur
Patella
Radius
Tibia
Ulna
Fibula
Carpus
Pisiform
Metacarpus
Metatarsus
Phalanges

(NB The Standard is quite clear about the sloping shoulders and yet one of the most common faults in our hounds is the set of the shoulder, which is so often very straight thus not allowing the necessary freedom of movement in front.)

Body *Topline straight and level. Chest well let down to below elbow. Ribs well sprung and extending well back. Short between the couplings. Loins powerful and supple, without excessive tuck-up.*

(NB The Standard requires the chest to be well let down to *below* elbow. This depth is so important for the make-up of the Beagle to allow him to have plenty of heart and lung room.)

Hindquarters *Very muscular about the thighs. Stifles well bent. Hocks firm, well let down and parallel to each other.*

(NB The Standard particularly says that the stifles should be well bent. A Beagle with straight stifles has no drive from behind and it is most important that he should have this motivation coming from his rear.)

Feet *Tight and firm. Well knuckled up and strongly padded.*

Not hare-footed. Nails short.

Gait *Back level and no roll. Stride free, long reaching and straight without high action. Hind legs showing drive. Should not move close behind or paddle or plait in front.*

(NB A slight turning in of the front feet, at the trot, in my opinion, should be allowed as this is the dog's natural inclination and helps him achieve balance.)

Tail *Sturdy and of moderate length. Set on high and carried gaily but not curled over back or inclined forward from the root. Well covered with hair, especially on underside.*

Coat *Short, dense and weatherproof.*

Colour *Any recognised hound colour other than liver. Tip of stern white.*

(NB Hound colours are recognised as follows:

Tricolour The most popular and the best known but no more correct than any of the others. This is a combination of black, white and tan. There are many variations of these three colours, but the most common is the black blanketed hound with tan on the head and neck, and white on the legs, foreface and tip of the tail. White can be spread over the back, breaking up the blanket, and a little white on the foreface certainly gives the hound a more attractive appearance. A hound with a solid tan head and foreface is apt to look a little bit sombre, although some people prefer it.

Tan/white The tan can range from any shade of lightish orange to a deep brick tan on a white background.

Lemon/white These dogs can be very attractive varying from very pale, almost cream, to approaching a strong lemon shade on a white background.

Black/white These are much more rare and as indicated they are black on a white background.

Mottled Firstly the *tricolour* which is black/white/tan with the addition of tan or black spots or flecks on the white parts of the body. *Blue mottled.* It is a tragedy that these seem to be dying out as they were so very attractive with their spots or flecks of blue appearing on the white of the legs or foreface.

Pied. Lemon Pied is made up of lemon hairs mixed in with white (usually more cream) and black hairs. When they are puppies it can often be noticed that a black streak runs down their back. This usually disappears as they get older. The black hairs do not appear in patches on pieds, they are quite separate and individual.

These photographs depict three hounds of excellent beagle type

Above:
Argentinian Champion Rossut Doubling
Best in show winner 1976

Top right:
Champion Rossut Foreman

Below right:
American Champion Jana Pagent
Best of breed Santa Barbara 1976

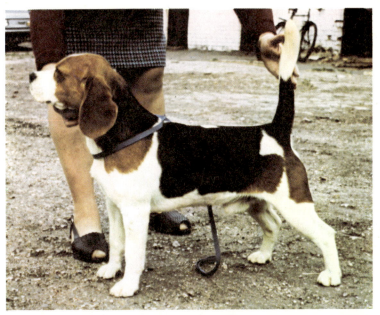

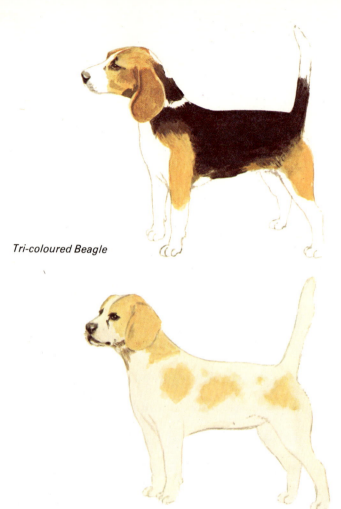

Tri-coloured Beagle

Lemon Beagle

Hare Pied Similar to the lemon pied except in place of the lemon colour is more a mixture of a brownish orange, like the hare itself, and mixed in with white, or again more correctly described as cream and grey and black.

Badger Pied This colour gives the impression of being a greyish hue. The background is white and the mixture is of black, cream and grey, resembling the badger.

The Standard condemns liver hounds and it is certainly not one of our most popular colours and discouraged in most sources. This colour usually produces a very horrid yellow eye colour which cannot give the kind, gentle expression so much desired. Invariably this colour also possesses a liver nose and the whole picture of the head is transformed into something quite foreign to the Beagle.

Occasionally one comes across an all white hound and, provided the pigmentation is correct, they can be rather attractive and are certainly acceptable.

I feel it is a pity that when the Standard was revised in 1973 no attempt was made to include in detail the above various colours of the Beagle.)

Weight and Size *It is desirable that height from ground to withers should neither exceed 16in. (41cm.) nor fall below 13in. (33cm.)*

Note: Male animals should have two apparently normal testicles fully descended into the scrotum.

The aforegoing Standard of the Beagle varies in small degrees from the American Standard and I give in detail the last mentioned, together with the defects as given by the American Kennel Club. The main difference is the question of size, and in the USA two different heights are acceptable and the Beagles are divided into these two varieties for the show ring.

The American Breed Standard

Head *The skull should be fairly long, slightly domed at occiput, with cranium broad and full.*

Ears *Set on moderately low, long, reaching when drawn out nearly, if not quite, to the end of the nose; fine in texture, fairly broad — with almost entire absence of erectile power — setting close to the head, with the forward edge slightly inturning to the cheek — rounded at tip.*

Eyes *Eyes large, set well apart — soft and houndlike — expression gentle and pleading; of a brown or hazel color.*

Muzzle *Of medium length — straight and square-cut — the stop moderately defined.*

Jaws *Level. Lips free from flews; nostrils large and open.*

Defects *A very flat skull, narrow across the top; excess of dome, eyes small, sharp and terrierlike, or prominent and*

Good profile

Good front

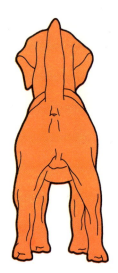

Good rear

Front faults

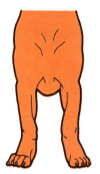

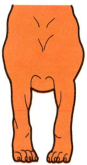

Feet turn out

Narrow fronted forward shoulders

Heavy shoulders feet toe in

Elbows out, barrel ribbed, spread feet

Rear faults

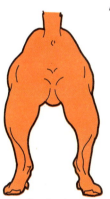
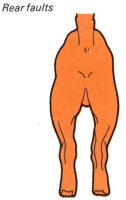
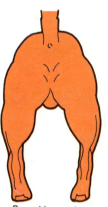

Cowhocked & dewclaws

Close behind and low tail

Barrel legged and too flabby

Faults in feet

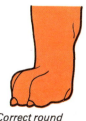
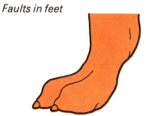

Correct round cat foot

Hare foot

Splay or spread foot

Tail faults

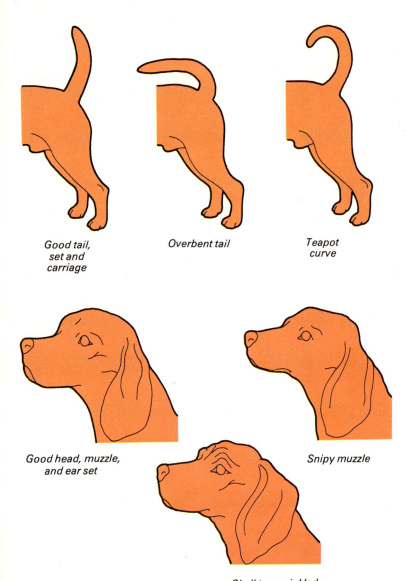

Good tail,
set and
carriage

Overbent tail

Teapot
curve

Good head, muzzle,
and ear set

Snipy muzzle

Skull too wrinkled,
ears too high

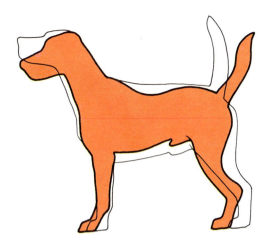

Solid shape indicates dog with typical faults, while outline shape indicates good shape by comparison

protruding; muzzle long, snipy or cut away decidedly below the eyes, or very short. Roman-nosed, or upturned, giving a dish-face expression. Ears short, set on high or with a tendency to rise above the point of origin.

Body. Neck and Throat *Neck rising free and light from the shoulders strong in substance yet not loaded, of medium length. The throat clean and free from folds of skin; a slight wrinkle below the angle of the jaw, however, may be allowable.* **Defects** *A thick, short, cloddy neck carried on a line with the top of the shoulders. Throat showing dewlap and folds of skin to a degree termed 'throatiness'.*

Shoulders and Chest *Shoulders sloping, clean, muscular, not heavy or loaded — conveying the idea of freedom of action with activity and strength. Chest deep and broad, but not broad enough to interfere with the free play of the shoulders.* **Defects** *Straight, upright shoulders. Chest disproportionately wide or with lack of depth.*

Back, Loin and Ribs *Back short, muscular and strong. Loin broad and slightly arched, and the ribs well sprung, giving abundance of lung room.* **Defects** *Very long or swayed or roached back. Flat, narrow loin. Flat ribs.*

Forelegs and Feet. Forelegs *Straight with plenty of bone in proportion to size of the hound. Pasterns short and straight.* **Feet** *Close round and firm. Pad full and hard.* **Defects** *Out at elbows. Knees knuckled over forward, or bent backward. Forelegs crooked or Dachshund-like. Feet long, open or spreading.*

Hips, Thighs, Hind Legs and Feet *Hips and thighs strong and well muscled, giving abundance of propelling power. Stifles strong and well let down. Hocks firm, symmetrical and moderately bent. Feet close and firm.* **Defects** *Cowhocks, or straight hocks. Lack of muscle and propelling power. Open feet.*

Tail *Set moderately high; carried gaily, but not turned forward over the back; with slight curve; short as compared with size of the hound; with brush.* **Defects** *A long tail. Teapot curve or inclined forward from the root. Rat tail with absence of brush.*

Coat *A close, hard, hound coat of medium length.* **Defects** *A short, thin coat, or of a soft quality.*

Color *Any true hound color.*

General Appearance *A miniature Foxhound, solid and big for his inches, with the wear-and-tear look of the hound that can last in the chase and follow his quarry to the death.*

Varieties *There shall be two varieties. Thirteen inch — which shall be for hounds not exceeding 13in. (33cm.) in height. Fifteen inch — which shall be for hounds over 13in. but not exceeding 15in. (38cm.) in height.*

Scale of Points

Head			Running Gear		
Skull	5		Forelegs	10	
Ears	10		Hips, thighs and		
Eyes	5		hind legs	10	
Muzzle	5	25	Feet	10	30
Body					
Neck	5		Coat	5	
Chest and			Stern	5	10
shoulders	15				
Back, loin and				Total	100
ribs	15	35			

Disqualification *Any hound measuring more than 15in. (38cm.) shall be disqualified.*

Choosing a puppy

There is only one place to buy a puppy and that is from the breeder. Certainly visit several kennels before you make your final choice, but do not side-track the issue and purchase your puppy from other than the home in which it was bred.

By visiting kennels you can judge immediately whether the puppy has come from a well managed kennel or a badly managed one. Never forget that the puppy's start in life is terribly important and it can only get this if the kennel management has been first class and it has had a good routine with good food and care.

A puppy with a good start in life is like a child that has been well brought up – they are a pleasure to call your own and one should be proud of them.

By visiting kennels you can judge how all the inmates appear, i.e. if they are in good coat and condition and if they look happy. You can always see the dam of your puppy and most times the sire, unless an outside stud dog has been used. All these things are important and can assure you, or not assure you, that your puppy is coming from a good background, clean and hygienic, and, from talking to the breeder, you will learn a great deal about how to cope with your puppy and also of the puppy's background.

To visit kennels you simply must make an appointment. Kennel owners are very busy people and the keeping of livestock is not just a 'nine to five' job. Most kennel owners will be delighted to show you over their kennels and to let you see their stock, but they do appreciate an appointment, and they do hope that if you make one, you will keep it. It is surprising how many people do not.

Names of reputable breeders can be had from the Kennel Club at 1 Clarges Street, Piccadilly, London W1. The telephone number is 01-493 6651. If you are purchasing in another country, the same information can be had from the Kennel Club of that country.

In Britain there are also two very good weekly dog magazines that list breeders' advertisements – *Our Dogs,* Oxford Road Station Approach, Manchester M60 1SX and *Dog World,* 32, New Street, Ashford, Kent. These are obtainable from any good newsagent.

Having made your appointment, you no doubt look forward

to the visit with great excitement. If you have a family, this is a great event for the children, but they must be asked to respect the puppy right from the word go. It is not a toy for them to play with when they feel like it and dismiss when they are tired of it. The puppy is to be a companion for them, and a good, loyal friend it will be if they are brought up together sensibly. They should give each other many years of great joy and friendship.

Before you visit the kennels, it is just as well to decide whether or not you intend to buy a dog or a bitch. I always feel that this is an entirely personal matter and the choice should be completely the new owners' and what suits them best. Both sexes make grand companions and never think, please, that the bitch will be a nuisance when she comes into season. There are many excellent preparations on the market today that can help her over this condition and, if perhaps you find it difficult to cope with unwelcome four-footed guests, there are many excellent kennels that will care for her during the height of her season. Do not be put off by this as the thrill of allowing her to have a litter when she is old enough knows no bounds, and once again is an excellent education for children. This is a charming and natural way of relating to your children how the young come into the world.

It is not an easy matter to make up your mind about a particular puppy and the breeder will not rush you into buying one until you are quite sure. Please do not touch the puppies, as at their early age they will not be injected against the many virus infections, and quite unintentionally you could be responsible for passing on some infection to them. The owner of the kennel will no doubt ask you not to touch the youngsters. Do not take exception to this for they are only protecting their own stock which could well have taken them many, many years to build up. There is a lot of time and a lot of hard work involved, to say nothing of the cost. Of course, once you have chosen your puppy, you will be perfectly entitled to hold him or her in your arms and have a good look at the new purchase.

Usually on seeing an audience, the puppies will tumble out of bed and run over to make friends. By watching the puppies you can soon tell whether they have good, happy temperaments or not. There might just be a little shy one among them, but so often these puppies, when given individual attention in a private home, blossom out and become great characters. If the puppy tends to run away and hide then I think you must be

Pet puppy with rubber bone

a little wary of its character, but if it settles when you have it in your arms, then I think you could win the battle of shyness.

The puppy should have clear, bright eyes. Beagle puppies have an enchanting gleam of mischief in their eyes and I assure you that it is not there for nothing! The nose of the puppy should be free from any sign of discharge and be comparatively cool to the touch. A Beagle's coat should be clean and glossy and there should be no sign of dandruff or skin problems. Its teeth should be clean and its breath sweet smelling. It should have been satisfactorily wormed before it leaves the breeder, and this is a routine job in a well run kennel. Every puppy has worms, or practically every puppy, and this is no disgrace to the kennel where it has been bred. Do not think that because worms are mentioned that it must be a mis-managed kennel. Its toenails should have been treated and they should be short and tidy. Toenails on young puppies are cut pretty regularly so that they do not inflict injuries on the dam. Once the puppies are running around on hard ground the toenails usually look after themselves.

The puppy's ears should be spotlessly clean and show no

signs of dirt or discharge. If a puppy appears a little lethargic, it may be that it has just wakened up and in no time at all it should be frolicking with its brothers and sisters.

It has probably been your intention to buy what the breeder might term 'a pet puppy', i.e. a puppy that does not quite come up to show standard, but nevertheless a puppy that is perfectly healthy and fit and very capable of giving you all the companionship that you desire. Never think that because the breeder has chosen to call them 'pet puppies' that they are not good. The standard of show dogs is so very high and breeders count themselves very fortunate indeed if they get one or two such specimens in one litter. The surplus obviously has to find pet homes, such as yours and many other people's. The reason for a puppy being classified as 'pet' could be for some minor fault, such as carrying its tail too gaily or being too long in the back or because the feet are not knuckled up enough. These are small faults that perhaps you would not even notice unless they were explained to you by the breeder. Most breeders will not object in the slightest to going over your puppy and explaining all the various points in detail. If you are genuinely interested, you will find that the breeder is too. In any case, what your puppy lacks in good looks he can well make up for in temperament and condition, and what more could you ask for in a pet puppy?

Puppies do not usually leave their breeder until they are about eight weeks of age. This move is a very bewildering time for puppies but usually Beagle babies settle in quite quickly. They are taken away from their usual routine and they have lost the hands that feed them. Even fresh smells appear and, instead of the good old kennel disinfectant, it now seems to them something quite different – perhaps even Christian Dior! The breeder should supply every new owner with a diet sheet and, if this is strictly adhered to, the transition period for the puppy should be made much easier. It has lots of new things to learn when it goes to a new home and if its meals can be very much the same as before, this will certainly help its digestion. So often puppies have slight digestive upsets and if this can be avoided so much the better.

It may be that with the car or train journey, the puppy will be upset and a little sick on its first journey home. If this is the case let the puppy settle before you try to give it either liquid or food. A little water with glucose added should be beneficial to it until it has time to settle down.

The puppy may be a lost little soul to begin with, and particularly so during the night when it will miss its brothers and sisters most. If it is inclined to be a little unsettled for the first two or three nights, leave it to get on with it. If you do not, you are making a rod for your own back as, even at this early age, a Beagle puppy will be intelligent enough to know that if it screams and gets attention, it is on to a good thing.

The dog will settle very quickly if it realises that no one is coming to sympathise with it and share its bed. Just make perfectly sure that, before you retire for the evening, all the puppy's comforts have been attended to and if it has a toy of its own, which it should have, put this in its box and, having given it a goodnight biscuit, leave it to its own devices. If you soften and take the puppy to your bedroom, it will adore this and will not easily be broken of it. Think of the adventures in the middle of the night and the attraction of a lovely slipper to chew or even a good battle with a rug. This will not be the puppy's fault but entirely yours – you have been warned. (See the section on basic training, page 44.)

Your breeder should have told you all about the injections that are required for your new charge. A great deal of time and money has been spent on perfecting these vaccines and I must advise you most strongly to have them done by your veterinary surgeon within a reasonable time of taking your puppy home. I always like to suggest that the puppy should have been allowed to explore and settle in its new home for about a week or ten days before it is subjected to its 'jabs'. During this period your puppy should not be taken out of the garden, and should be protected from all other dogs until it is certified fit to be social by the veterinary surgeon. The course of injections is usually two, with a fortnight between them and there is very seldom any reaction. The puppy has a natural immunity while with its mother but, when it leaves the kennels, it is really wide open to the many virus infections that could lurk round the corner. Be safe and keep the puppy isolated in your home until it has its protection.

A young puppy requires a great deal of sleep in its early life and on no account should it be disturbed while it is resting. The children must wait until it stirs from its sleep, and likewise the puppy must never disturb the children's sleep by barking or screaming or scratching at the door. Bringing up children with a puppy can be a marvellous way of teaching discipline to both parties.

When you take your puppy away from the kennels, the breeder should give you a copy of its pedigree. This gives the background of your puppy for about five generations. If the puppy is registered with the Kennel Club, the breeder must give you a form transferring the puppy from the breeder to you. If the puppy is not registered with the Kennel Club, then the breeder must give you a signed form so that you can personally register the puppy with the Kennel Club. If you have purchased a bitch puppy then it is essential that you have her registered, just in case in time you decide to let her have a litter. If you have bought a dog there is no need to register it with the Kennel Club but it is rather nice to think that it is registered with that élite body.

It is a common habit for the layman to tell his friends that his dog has a pedigree as long as his arm and even longer. You will see from the history of the Beagle that every dog today registered could have a pedigree more than a mile long. This is not the point. It is far more important that the dogs in the pedigree should be of first class stock and that they have more virtues than faults. The relationship of the dogs in the pedigree is also of vital importance.

All dogs in Great Britain must have a licence from the age of six months onwards and these licences are obtainable at your local post office.

Show puppy

All the foregoing applies to a show prospect puppy but, in choosing this puppy, there is the need for greater care and attention to the Standard Points of the Breed. It is no good purchasing a show puppy if, for instance, its mouth and teeth are not correct, or if it has not got good round bone. Read the Standard very carefully and read all available literature on the breed. Go to a show and see what the breeders are showing, speak to them and learn something about the breed, watch the winning kennels at the show and make an appointment with them. You will see by the show catalogues who the good breeders are and how successful they are. Having chosen the kennel that you wish to visit, go armed with questions and if the breeder cannot answer the majority satisfactorily, then I feel that you are not quite on the right road. Try another kennel and take time to choose your first show puppy. All good breeders and genuine lovers of the breed will be only too happy to help you. They are just as proud when you win something with their stock as they are when they themselves are successful.

Of course your show puppy will cost more than a pet puppy and the price will depend on its age when you buy it. My advice is to buy the best that you can afford at an age when you can see what it is going to grow into, and this is usually about five or six months for a Beagle. Many people choose a show puppy well before this age, but the longer one can leave it, the more likely it is that nothing will go wrong as far as teeth, make, shape and temperament are concerned. Naturally, a puppy at five or six months of age will be much more expensive than a hopeful at three months. There is the question of Mother Nature and what she can do and what she cannot do to take into consideration. There always has to be that little bit of luck in breeding livestock.

Whether you are purchasing a show puppy or just a good companion, I hope that your first Beagle will give you as much pleasure and happiness as all mine have given to me.

General care

Feeding

Beagles are tough, sturdy little hounds and not faddy eaters and, provided they are fed sensibly, they should be no trouble in this respect. If anything, they are much more inclined to over-eat, and this must be watched very carefully so that you do not end up with a fat roly-poly monster. This is particularly important at the puppy stage when the bone is soft and not properly set. If the puppy has to carry too much weight, it is quite likely that, by carrying this extra flesh, the formation of its legs will suffer, and you could well finish up with a bandy-legged hound. There is a tremendous amount of common sense in the rearing of any puppy and I give herewith a diet that should help to keep you on the right road in respect of your Beagle's meals.

Up to 14 weeks

8 a.m.	3 – 4oz. (85-114g.) raw meat plus brown bread and gravy or a fine biscuit meal.
12 noon	About half a cupful of baby cereal.
4 p.m.	As at 8 a.m.
8 p.m.	Milk with honey added.

14 weeks to 6 months

8 a.m.	4 – 6oz. (114-170g.) raw meat plus brown bread and gravy or a terrier-size biscuit meal.
12 noon	Baby cereal or something similar with an egg added twice a week and on the other days honey added.
6 p.m.	As at 8 a.m.

6 months to a year

8 a.m.	6 – 8 oz. (170-227g.) raw meat plus brown bread and gravy or biscuit meal.

Drink of milk at lunch time.

6 p.m.	As at 8 a.m.

The puppy can be given additional calcium in the form of a bone meal powder, which is available from any good pet shop. Make sure this bone meal is for animal consumption and not for use on the garden, etc.

A good feeding bowl

Always soak any meal before it is given to your Beagle. If not previously soaked, meal can swell up inside the dog and cause great discomfort.

It is essential that fresh, clean water is available for your Beagle at all times. This should be kept in the same place or places so that very soon it will know where to have a drink if and when it requires it.

Never leave any uneaten food about. Flies have a nasty habit of descending on this and leaving their mark, and they are not the cleanest of insects. Apart from this, it is a very bad habit to allow your puppy to eat at its convenience. When it has been given a reasonable time to eat its meal, and it begins to pick at it, then is the time to take it away. This will teach it not to be lazy or slovenly over its food. To allow this can create a very bad habit and must be stopped right at the beginning.

To vary the diet, a fish meal can be substituted for a meat

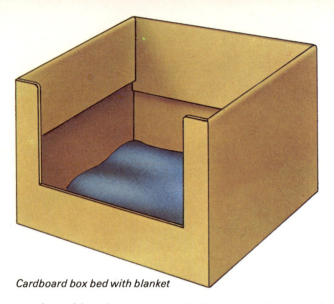

Cardboard box bed with blanket

meal, and herrings are particularly good in vitamin value. A hard biscuit to go to bed with is not only permissible but helps the animal to settle down for the night, and as it grows older it will look forward to this special little treat.

If, for any reason, raw meat is not available or too costly, any of the prepared frozen meats for animal consumption are good substitutes and these are readily available from a good pet store or sometimes from your local butcher.

Housing

For a companion puppy it is usual for this to be housed inside your own home and, in this case, the puppy's requirements are minimal. I do not advise expensive baskets or beds until the puppy is a little older, as it is quite normal for the puppy to become bored when left on its own and resort to a good chewing session. A cardboard box can suffice until it has outgrown these habits, and it will be perfectly happy in this with a small blanket or even an old jersey to lie on.

If it is a truly naughty puppy and decides to have a party when everyone has gone to bed, and tear up linoleum or anything else in the room that it can get a hold of, then it is best to have a proper little box for it with a door that shuts, and it can then be locked in when it is left alone. (See the section on basic training, page 44.)

No doubt the box will be kept in the kitchen or a utility room, but wherever it is, it should be draught free, and this also applies if the Beagle has to sleep in an outhouse. It is essential that in the winter it should be kept warm but, as the Beagle is normally a very sturdy little dog, there is no need to pamper it. If it is kept in an outhouse in the winter, the box or bed should have an ample supply of wood shavings or straw and it will love to snuggle into this and make its own bed. If you do intend to keep your Beagle outside, always remember that it is unwise to have it in the heat of the house during the day and then turn it out at night. For a pet or companion it is much better to find some little corner for the dog and its bed inside the house.

For breeding stock or show stock we have wooden kennels surrounded by large runs. In these kennels are benches about 2 ft. (61cm.) off the ground and these are the sleeping quarters for the hounds. We usually run about four Beagles together and, on these benches, they snuggle up and sleep contentedly. In the winter the hounds have good straw on their benches to

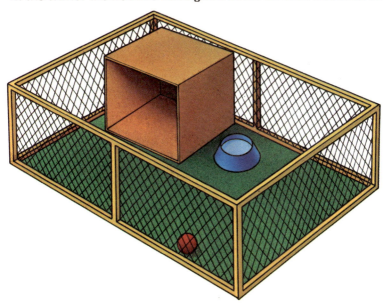

Outdoor puppy pen with water bowl and box

Three to four months

Mature Beagle

The growing Beagle

Eight week old puppy

Beagle puppies in kennel run

sleep on. This is renewed as soon as it becomes rather flattened and soiled. On the floor sawdust is used and this is renewed daily. The runs are part concrete and part cinders and ashes and we find that this keeps the Beagles' nails in excellent condition and their feet tight and firm. Kennel doors are kept open all day except in exceptionally bad weather and the Beagles can come and go as they please. Bedtime (when the kennel doors are shut), is about 8 p.m. or even later in the hot evenings in the summer. During the winter as soon as nightfall approaches the Beagles take to their beds and are usually bedded down by about 5 or 6 p.m., or even earlier if it is a nasty old night. The hounds are let out in the morning at about 7 a.m. and, with a regular routine, they keep their kennels incredibly clean.

The runs are surrounded by 6ft. (1.83m.) chain link, heavy gauge fencing which is concreted into the ground. This prevents the hounds deciding to dig out and join their neighbours, and there are very few Beagles that will climb over a 6ft. (1.83m.) fence. I have known one bitch that climbed like a monkey, but she was rather the exception, thank goodness. Fresh water, of course, is always available and adequate shade must be given from the sun.

Large wooden platforms about 2-3ft. (61-91cm.) off the ground are placed in the runs and the Beagles delight in jumping on and off these obstacles, strengthening their quarters as they take this exercise. It is not unusual to see four or five Beagles trying to sun themselves on the top of one of these platforms that are really only big enough to take three – a comical sight! Being active little people, the Beagles enjoy these large runs where they can take as much exercise as they wish and enjoy many a game of hide-and-seek.

Exercise

As will be seen from the above the show Beagle kept under these conditions requires very little more exercise except, of course, its lead training for the show ring, and controlled road exercise. The latter is most important as it uses and tunes up muscles that are not used in the galloping exercises that the dog takes on its own. Also the controlled walk or trot gait is what is expected of it in the show ring and it teaches it to control its balance on the move and to be obedient to its handler's commands.

The old saying of *'As a dog moves, so is he built'*, is so very true.

The house pet takes a great deal of its own exercise by just trotting after its master or mistress in the home or by playing with the children in the garden, but it too must have its controlled exercise, and over and above this, if possible, it must be able to have some good, free galloping.

Until a Beagle puppy is about four months of age, it needs little more than the exercise it will get at home and, as already

A transportation cage

mentioned, it certainly should not be taken outside its own home to exercise until it has had its full course of injections.

Like the show puppy it can then advance to controlled walks on the lead and some free exercise on the common. Until it is trained to come back to its owner, it should not be allowed off its lead and to give the free exercise, it is as well to put it on a very long rope and let it gallop wherever it feels like going.

A mature Beagle must have this free exercise plus its road exercise otherwise it will get bored with the confines of its garden and home, and this spells trouble.

Basic training
Let us take the companion puppy first, as it has a slightly different upbringing from that of the show puppy. The first thing to teach both, however, is to know their name and to respond to it.

Always be kind but firm with your puppy in training and one must have great patience, particularly in the early stages. Never ever punish or scold a dog unless you have caught it in the act and are absolutely sure that it is the guilty party. Never hit with your hand, for the dog knows your hand as the thing that pets and pats it and produces food for it. To chastise with this nice hand bewilders the animal and it becomes very wary, even afraid of it. A rolled-up newspaper is a very effective weapon and a little gentle hit on its backside with this makes it quickly understand that whatever it has done is not quite right.

The first real essential in a house pet is to teach it to be clean and this should not present any real difficulties. Be firm and be patient and you should be rewarded quite quickly. The puppy should, of course, be put outside to relieve itself as soon as it has finished its meal. When it does this, praise it with your voice and tell it what a good dog it has been. It is perhaps easier to housetrain a puppy in the summer months when it is so easy to open the door and put it out without letting in the cold blasts of winter, and naturally these cold blasts are not very welcome to the puppy either. It too would prefer to stay inside and relieve itself but it must learn that this is not right. Paper can be used to help over this difficult period. Spread a newspaper out in a corner of the floor and it will soon realise that this is the place to spend its money. If it attempts to do it on the floor, just lift it gently and put it on the newspaper and, when it has performed, praise it well. The newspaper can gradually be

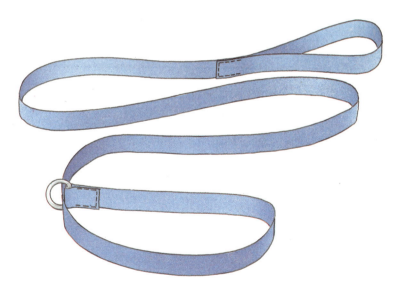

Lightweight slip lead

moved right to the door, and eventually it can be thrown outside, and the puppy should understand that is the place where it must go.

With a very stubborn puppy that insists upon making a mess on the floor, particularly during the night, it is a very good idea to shut it up in a box as described in the section on housing, page 38. The puppy will not want to dirty its own house and very rarely will you find it anything but clean in the morning. It may make a mistake to begin with, but it will find it so distasteful that it is unlikely to recur, and this is an excellent way of training the more difficult ones.

Regularity of meals and general routine is very important and once your Beagle knows what belongs to it, such as its own bed or box, its own toys, etc. it should never be permitted to play or tamper with anything else. Be quite firm about this otherwise the puppy could become a menace in your household. It may be rather amusing to see a toilet roll unravelled all round the house (I have a Griffon that adores to do just this when she can), but it is not so funny when things go a bit further and mother's knitting is attacked with dire results. Your Beagle will be just as happy as a disciplined member of the community as it will be as an undisciplined one.

When your puppy has got to know you and to know its name and is nearly housetrained, then is the time to start to lead train it. First of all put a very lightweight collar round its neck, and this should be done when you are there to observe its reactions. I am a firm believer that no collar should be kept on a dog permanently. There are many things that a collar can latch on to and, in the dog's desperation to get clear, there can be disastrous results. This particularly applies to a choke collar — you have been warned!

When the puppy seems quite happy with the collar, then is the time to attach a very light lead. It may resent this intensely and behave like a bucking bronco. Pay no regard to these antics, be firm, placate the dog, speak to it gently and settle it down. It will soon realise that these antics get it nowhere. Don't pull but try to lead the dog firmly and gently, talking to it all the time by simply saying, 'Good dog or good whatever the name is,' and generally encourage it with kind words. Never lose your temper for it will only confuse the puppy and all your efforts will be in vain. This exercise must never be treated as a game. It must be taken very seriously by both of you and,

The correct way to put a choke-chain on a young Beagle

please, during this training session it must always be the same person who teaches the dog, as if it has several handlers at this stage it will be very confused. Once the dog walks on the lead then, of course, the whole family can have their turns but always with patience and kindness, until it accepts the whole routine as commonplace.

As the dog gets older and goes outside for its walks, and meets more interesting smells, it may be that it will want to ponder over these smells and be reluctant to behave properly. This can very quickly be controlled by the use of a choke chain. As the dog pulls to one side to get its own way, a quick jerk on

Walking to heel on a choke-chain

Teaching puppy to 'stand', using a delicacy to attract and hold his attention

the choke chain will being it back to the realisation that it must come when you want it to come. This is particularly important when it meets another of its fellow canines and you certainly do not want it hob-nobbing with all and sundry. You must ensure that when you put the choke chain round the neck that you put it on correctly so that the lead will loosen when you loosen your hold.

As it grows older, the dog will graduate to longer walks and freedom from the lead, but, before you are able to let it off the lead in the park or the common, you must be absolutely certain that it will not chase poultry, sheep or cattle, or a rider on horseback. If found chasing livestock, the dog is liable to be shot and you will have no legal redress.

As far as a show puppy's training is concerned this is given

A reluctant dog can be taught to 'come' with the use of a long lead

in detail in the chapter on Exhibiting and Show Training. In kennels, promising show stock are usually left to grow up with as little fuss as possible. They have a very strict routine as far as their feeding, cleaning, grooming, etc. is concerned and they are handled as much as possible by the kennel staff and owner, so that when they come under the hand of the judge they are not unduly perturbed by it. They lead a very happy life with their kennel companions, some from one litter and some from another, while the anxious breeder watches over them, wondering all the time whether these precious puppies are going to fulfil their early promise, or default in some small way which takes them out of the show bracket and into the companion group. As Somerville said: 'Select with Judgement.' Often it is easier said than done.

A puppy can be taught to 'sit' in this way. Holding the food bowl at mealtimes you can gently push the hindquarters down

Grooming

Beagles require very little grooming and in this respect they are very well suited to those of us who do not care to compete with long coats which need constant attention and can be very time consuming. Because of this it is surprising that occasionally we find in the show ring a Beagle that looks more dirty than even reasonably clean and without any gloss on its coat. This is an insult to the judge involved and should never happen. No animals that are kept in a dirty condition can ever be happy in themselves and it is unfair not to give them the little attention that they need in this respect.

A rubber glove or good stiff brush are excellent aids to keeping the coat clean and healthy and getting rid of all old hairs. The dog should be groomed every day and particularly a hound with a harsher and thicker coat. Old hair must be got rid of and it is just not possible for the dog to shake this off itself.

Beagles should not be bathed too often as this tends to get rid of the natural oil in the coat. Of course, you must bath it if it has rolled in some savoury piece of dirt while out exercising, as the stench coming from its coat could well drive one out of house and home. Do see that the bath is not too hot for it; tepid water is perfectly satisfactory. Make sure that you have everything that you require for this operation before you start, as if you have to leave the dog in the bath for one moment while you snatch a towel or soap, you can be sure that it will be off shaking itself violently in all directions. There are very many excellent shampoos on the market and these are available at your pet shop. Do be careful to keep the soapy water out of the eyes and, of course, the ears. Beagles can have trouble with their ears. If you see the dog scratching them on the outside, you must look further for the trouble inside and, if they are rather filthy with a blackish, horrid-smelling substance, take the dog off to your veterinary surgeon for proper treatment. Never poke in a dog's ears. They are very sensitive and without knowing what you are doing you can do untold damage. If you take the patient off for veterinary advice the ears will soon clear and you will have a happier dog.

Nails should be inspected to make sure that they have not grown too long. If you are giving your Beagle the correct sort of exercise, it is unlikely that these should give any trouble at all once the dog is out of puppyhood. There are several very good

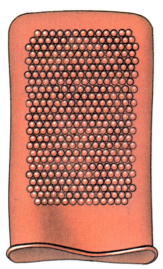

Rubber grooming glove

Guillotine type nail clippers

Fine metal comb

Grooming equipment

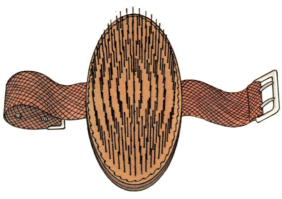

Cushioned wire pad for brushing out the coat

Stripping knife – only to be used to tidy the tail

Groom daily with a rubber hound glove.

types of nail scissors or clippers available. I prefer the guillotine type because they are easy to use and one can see exactly what one is cutting off. Do be careful not to cut the quick as this can be very painful to the dog. This is most important in show dogs, as when the judge examines the feet, you do not want the dog to think that he is going to attack its nails and that the whole business will be painful.

Teeth must be watched and particularly when the first teeth are being discarded, as it sometimes happens that the puppy incisors are reluctant to leave. If the second teeth appear to be coming in rather unevenly due to the presence of the first teeth, then do ask your veterinary surgeon to help in this matter. If the puppy is a show puppy, it is most important that it should have no unpleasant memories of teeth being extracted otherwise it will be very loath to show its teeth and mouth to the judge. In this case, it is much better that anything that has to be done to the mouth should be done under an anaesthetic and your veterinary surgeon will be able to advise on this.

Tartar may collect on your Beagle's teeth as it approaches old age. Once again your veterinary surgeon should be asked to scale them and make them clean. If you allow your Beagle to eat hard biscuits, and perhaps even a marrow bone, it is unlikely that it will have dirty teeth until its rather advanced years.

With regard to any trimming of the show Beagle, I am not in favour of anything more than just tidying it up. This is a very natural little dog and it horrifies me to know that some people have cut off its whiskers to make its face look cleaner. Whiskers are the dog's defence against flies and other pests and nature meant that they should be left on. No judge of any hound breed would consider a head improved by this cosmetic performance.

I have even seen Beagles shaved to give their neck a clean look, and to me this is quite monstrous. If the hair under the pads happens to grow excessively, then I feel it is quite

Use a strong bath with warm water and have all necessary accessories to hand

permissible to trim this with scissors, purely for the dog's own comfort. The tip of the stern can be plucked with finger and thumb to give a neat finish, but under no circumstances should scissors be used.

Nearly all show Beagles have their dew claws removed and this is one part of cosmetic surgery that I heartily agree with. This is done when the puppy is about three days old and causes no upset whatsoever. It gives a cleaner line to the legs and as dew claws serve no useful purpose, they are just as well removed. They have a nasty habit of catching on stockings or clothes, or in the undergrowth when the puppy is having its free exercise. A torn dew claw can cause the Beagle a lot of unnecessary pain and they do bleed rather excessively.

In the olden days it was said that the dew claws were put there for a purpose and that purpose was to allow the dog to keep its teeth clean. I prefer our present day methods.

The benching chain

Exhibiting and show training

Exhibiting

Before one attempts to exhibit, it is wise to attend several shows and get to know what it is all about. There are shows in every part of the country most weekends and very often during the week. Details of these shows can be found in the weekly dog magazines.

In Britain there are three types of show ranging from the Championship Shows at the top of the tree, to the Open Shows, and so down the scale to the Limited Shows. The Limited Shows, as the name suggests, are shows where the entry is limited to members of clubs or societies, or to exhibitors within specified areas. These shows are much smaller than the Open Shows but are very well supported and are ideal for taking a puppy out for the first time, for new exhibitors and for beginner judges.

If you wish to exhibit at a show, the first step is to get a copy of the schedule from the secretary of the show concerned. The schedule is the contract between the exhibitor and the show and it contains all the necessary information. Read it very carefully and, more important, fill in the entry form even more carefully. Make sure that once your entry form is filled in, you post it in good time before the closing date of entries.

If the show is a benched show, i.e. the dogs are attached to separate benches, you will require a blanket plus a benching chain. All the incidentals that are required for a show dog are available at the shows at the various stands or stalls and, if you visited a benched show before you actually exhibited, you would acquaint yourself with all the necessities. Before you take your dog to a benched show, it is a very good idea to have a little practice at home. Put a benching chain on your Beagle by attaching it to a leather or nylon collar. Never use a choke collar for obvious reasons. Attach the end of the benching chain to a tree in the garden or even a table leg in the house and your Beagle will soon realise that its movements are restricted to a very small area. This helps it to settle on the bench at the show but do be patient with it for the first time or two. Your dog will be surrounded by many other dogs all in similar circumstances and it is amazing how quickly these show dogs accept the whole situation. When you have it settled on the bench, offer a drink of water, or milk if it prefers that. Watch the

Some shows are benched with this general arrangement

old hands and how they settle their dogs down, and you will soon get the picture yourself.

Very few dogs are unhappy on their benches and this is evidenced by the speed with which the experienced hounds jump on to their bench and settle down. If your dog is a bad traveller, it would be wise to let it settle on the bench for a reasonable period before you offer anything to drink or eat. You must judge your time of arrival at the show according to your own dog's individual requirements. If the dog is a bad traveller, then you must make sure that you arrive in plenty of time to allow it to settle down, and don't forget that you will want to give that little bit of extra spit and polish before you take it into the ring.

Having got your dog organised, you then settle down to await your call to the ring. All details of what is happening at the show will be found in the catalogue which is on sale at the show — never before. Check that your entry is included in the catalogue and if not, hurry off to the Secretary and enquire as to who has made a mistake. It could be the Secretary, it could be the printer, but it could be you.

If the show is not benched, you can either bring your Beagle into the hall to sit quietly at your side on its rug, or to the side of the ring if it is an out-of-doors show, or you can leave the dog in the car unless the weather makes this unbearable. You must teach it not to be argumentative with the other show dogs and it should be a model of good behaviour at all times. If you take your dog into a hall, please do see that it has had every opportunity to relieve itself before it goes indoors. Dogs make occasional mistakes but they must be given every chance to be clean.

When you enter the ring you will be given your ring number by a steward and told where to stand. Join the other exhibitors and make friends with them, because it is from them that you will learn about showing your dog. Do not start to chatter to them just as they are about to show their dog to the judge. They will be concentrating on their Beagle and will not want to be disturbed at this stage. Try not to be nervous. This may be a difficult thing to ask, as many of our very experienced exhibitors still feel that bit of tension, particularly at the Championship Shows. Tension can run down the lead and upset your Beagle and, although our little hounds are very tough people, they have very sensitive hearing and strange noises can be very distracting to them.

Most judges prefer to inspect Beagles on the table and you should have practised this at home from an early age. Few Beagles resent being put on a table, particularly if they have been trained to do this. After the table inspection, the judge will ask you to move your dog either up and down or in a triangle. Listen to what the judge has to say and do accordingly. There is nothing more infuriating to a judge than to ask an exhibitor specifically to move his hound in a triangle

The correct show stance for a puppy

and to find that instead the dog is being moved straight up and back. I like to see all dogs move in a triangle when I am judging, as not only can I see the dog come and go but I can also see his outline in profile. Having moved your dog, go back to your place in the ring and await the verdict. Most judges will bring out for final selection four or five dogs and, if you are lucky, you may even end up at the top of the list. It may be, however, that this particular judge does not share your opinion of your dog and that you leave the ring empty-handed.

If you are in the next class, the ring steward will indicate where you should stand and, although you may not have won anything in the previous class, it is quite wrong for you not to compete in the next class if you have entered. You can only be excused this class by special permission of the judge, and I can assure you that unless you have very special reasons for not going into your second or even third class, it is inadvisable not to attend. Remember there is always another day and another judge.

The judge is the all-important person on the day and most judges are kind and considerate to new puppies and to new handlers. Speak to the judge only if he or she speaks to you and, as already said, try to do as the judge asks without question. In this country today our entries are so large that the judge's time is precious and anything that tends to hinder decisions and waste time is not appreciated, not only by the judge but by the show management.

As far as training your Beagle is concerned there are two methods of showing. One is the loose lead, i.e. when the handler stands away from the dog and allows it to show on its own for a titbit. This is by far the best method but few people practise it, perhaps because it takes time to train the Beagle to show like this, but possibly because few dogs, of any sort, are natural showmen. When one gets one that will stand out and show on its own, it is indeed a great asset and a great joy to be at the other end of the lead.

I have already told you in what method most judges like their dogs to move and it is up to you to practise this at home and get it as near to perfection as possible. Certainly, discipline your Beagle to move as you want it to move and not the way it wants to move. If you can go one further and train it to show on a loose lead, looking up at you and paying attention to your instructions, then you are well on your way to becoming a good handler.

Exhibiting and showing dogs is a marvellous sport and, once you have been introduced to it, I am sure you will find it exhilarating and exciting. Of course, it has its not so good moments when you think you might have been higher placed than you were, but everyone has to learn to take the good with the bad and, after all, the judge did not ask you to show under him or her. You made the choice and went for a particular opinion and whether you like it or not is quite another matter. At least you will know not to show under that particular judge again, at least with that particular Beagle.

Table

"New" dogs (unseen by Judge)

Handler

Judge Dog being examined by Judge

"Old" dogs (already seen by Judge in a previous class)

Table

Judge

All dogs

"Once round, please"

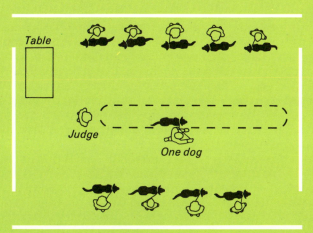

"Once up and down, please"

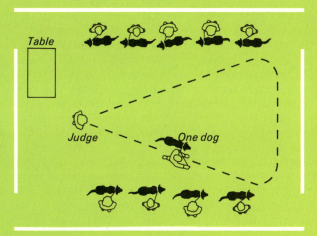

"Triangle, please"

Breeding

Breeding is without doubt the most exciting part of keeping dogs. Breeders will talk far into the night as to which dog they are going to mate to which bitch and which bloodlines they consider right and which not so good. There is one thing quite certain and that is that one must have a definite programme worked out and stick quite solidly to it. It is no good being put off this programme by someone trying to persuade you to use the latest champion dog or even the latest imported dog. (We have several American imported Beagles in the country.) If these dogs do not tie in with your dog's pedigree, then it is just a question of hit and miss.

I am a great believer in line breeding. This is the breeding of two animals that are related but not as closely related as inbreeding. I happily mate half-sister to half-brother or grandfather to grand-daughter and vice versa. I feel that this is the only way to establish one's type as one sees it according to the Standard, and to improve one's stock. Of course, there is always the odd flash in the pan from completely unrelated pedigrees but how often do these stars themselves really reproduce anything worthwhile? If one checks back, very seldom indeed.

If you are starting from scratch, study very carefully the Beagle that you like according to your interpretation of the Standard and, with this picture in mind, purchase a line-bred bitch, if you can, that fits into your picture. When the time comes to mate this bitch, you should select a dog of her own type and with the same good overall qualities that she has. He might not be a champion. In several breeds we have outstanding stud dogs that never did well in the ring, usually because they disliked it so very much. Carefully weigh up the pros and cons of both dog and bitch and give the whole question very careful thought. It is not only the appearance of an animal that matters but what lies behind the pedigree and it is a great help, of course, if you can remember what every animal in the pedigree looks like and what were their virtues and their faults. Our old-established breeders, who can remember the backgrounds of pedigrees, are usually only too happy to help the more novice breeders if they are really genuinely interested. It is a most fascinating study and one that is most time absorbing.

Any breeding stock should be free from outstanding faults and should be of the highest quality. Fortunately in Beagles we have very few problems and no serious hereditary faults. Nevertheless, it is unwise to breed from a bitch with a bad mouth or a dog with a curly stern. By a bad mouth I mean a jaw that is either undershot or overshot or a wry jaw. All these faults will be passed on, if not in the next generation, then in the one after that. Other faults such as heavy heads and bulgy eyes are not really in the best interests of the breed, just as poor bone and straight shoulders are undesirable. We must all try to improve our Beagles not just to perpetuate them.

A bitch usually comes into season when she is between eight and ten months old but, of course, she is not anything like mature at this age and should never be bred from until at least her second season. This gives you plenty of time to have well and truly considered the right mate for her.

If a show bitch is winning well and in sight of becoming a champion, she is often not bred from until she is about three years of age. Most bitches go neatly back into shape after a litter, but there is always the chance that her show lines might not be as beautiful as they were before her litter and so it is as well to campaign a good show bitch to her championship, if you can, before mating her. On the other hand, some bitches are very slow to mature and, by letting these bitches have a litter, they deepen in body and are much better for having their family. This all depends on the bitch herself and this has to be decided by the breeder.

A bitch is usually ready for mating about the eleventh to fourteenth day of her season but this can vary enormously and I have known bitches that have stood to be mated on their second or third day and they have had puppies. Equally at the other end of the line, bitches can stand up to their twentieth day and have successful litters. A bitch will usually let you know when she is ready by taking a great interest in any dog that happens to be around. The normal sign is for her to stand with her stern to one side welcoming the dog. Some bitches pretend that they do not want to be mated and snap and scream at the dog. As the stud dog owner has no wish to have the dog bitten, or themselves for that matter, the usual procedure with a difficult bitch is to tape her mouth until a mating has been effected. Thereafter, she is usually quite delighted about the whole thing and only too happy to stand quietly by the dog without a tape on. Bitches can be so wily but an experienced stud dog is never put off by their antics.

The gestation period is sixty-three days after the mating and during this period the bitch should be given extra food so that her whelps will get the benefit of it. Rather than give her more food all in one meal, it is wise to split it into two meals and, during the end of her period, even to three meals. If she has a big litter, she will not have quite the same space to put her food, and it is much more comfortable for her if this is given in smaller quantities. Her meat ration should be increased and her biscuit meal cut down slightly. An egg or two during the week is most beneficial and she should always have a plentiful supply of fresh water. She may whelp a day or two early or a day or two late but, provided she is not distressed, there is nothing to worry about. Maiden bitches can be a little more anxious about the whole thing than the more experienced matrons.

The bitch should be introduced to her whelping box about ten days before her due date. The box must be large enough for her to turn round comfortably and, about 2in. (5cm.) from the floor, there should be a rail round the box. This allows the puppies to be protected when the bitch lies down and can save a whelp or two from being crushed by the bitch if she has a big litter or gets a little bit fussed about the whole thing.

During the first four or five weeks of being in whelp the bitch should be allowed to take her normal exercise. It is about this time that you will definitely be able to detect the signs of pregnancy. Some bitches keep one guessing right up to the last week but the majority have ample proof by about the fifth week. From about the sixth to seventh week, they should steady up a bit in exercise and it is not very good for them at this stage to be bouncing up and down stairs. This probably gives the whelps a pretty rough passage, so do avoid this if possible. We tend to let them please themselves as far as exercise is concerned but it is most important that they should be kept in good physical condition for the job ahead of them.

Most breeders find newspapers the best material for whelping a bitch on. Her natural reaction as she draws close to her due date is to get into her box and tear away at the newspaper until it is all in shreds. She may repeat this several days running before she eventually settles down to whelp. Her whelping quarters and box should be kept scrupulously clean

The genital organs

Dog

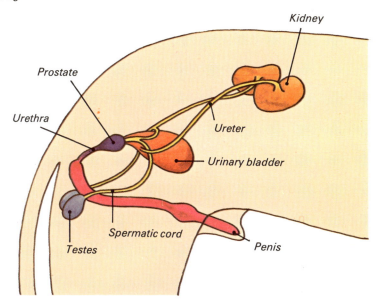

Kidney

Prostate

Urethra

Ureter

Urinary bladder

Spermatic cord

Testes

Penis

Bitch

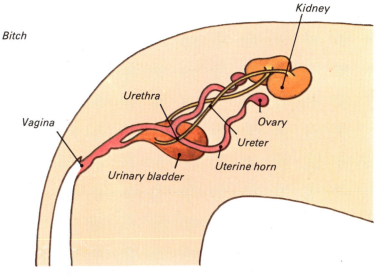

Kidney

Urethra

Ovary

Vagina

Ureter

Uterine horn

Urinary bladder

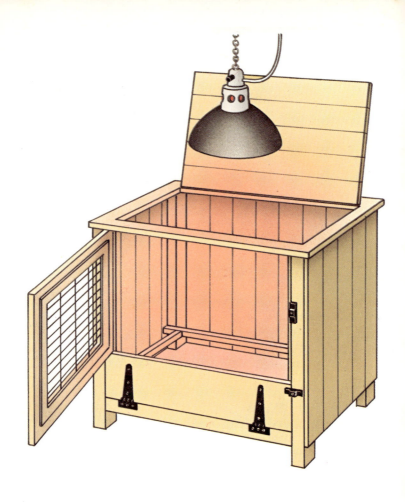

The whelping box, which will be newspaper lined can have either type of heating. Above is an infra-red lamp while below is shown an under box heater

at all times and the temperature in her kennel, or wherever she is whelping, should be around 70°F (21°C).

The first true signs of labour are when you actually see the bitch strain. If her temperature is taken at this stage it should have fallen to about 2°F below normal. Normal temperature is 101.5°F (38.5°C). The bitch should continue to strain at regular intervals and, when this becomes more frequent and increases in intensity, a water bag should appear. During all this time the bitch should be carefully observed, quite unobtrusively and without disturbing her. She is well able to get on with the job herself and she may quite easily resent any outside help. If you are keeping an eye on her and you feel that things are not going correctly, then you are there to lend a hand or to call for veterinary help. Without lots of experience never try to help the bitch yourself. It is far better to get professional help rather than be sorry afterwards.

If everything is going well, give her a little hot milk between the whelps or, in winter, a spot of hot gruel is usually much appreciated. If she has a big litter, and Beagles can have up to ten or eleven puppies, it is as well to try to change the paper with as little bother as possible so that her bed remains comparatively dry. In my own kennels we find that the under box strip heater is a marvellous help in keeping the bed dry and keeping the whelps warm. During whelping, particularly in the colder weather, infra-red lamps supply heat from above the bitch, but I do not like to use these for too long as I find that after a week or so the whelps' coats become a little too dry and this encourages scurf. I prefer to shut the lid of the whelping box, keep the under box heater going and put plenty of wood-wool round the bitch and puppies. In using these electrical appliances great care must be made to ensure, as far as possible, that the bitch cannot get to the wires which she might chew in her anxiety before whelping.

Handle the whelps as little as possible otherwise you will upset the dam and make her restless, and she will try and cover them with paper or pick them up in her mouth and walk round her box with them. If she does this she is obviously disturbed by your presence and it is best to leave her alone and, if possible, watch her from outside the room through a window.

When she has finished whelping, she must be persuaded to leave her family and go for a walk in the garden. Put a lead on her and take her out very gently. She will be reluctant to go but go she must, as she should relieve herself and make herself more comfortable. As each puppy is born there is an afterbirth attached and most bitches prefer to eat this as they break off the cord. This is perfectly all right for her to do but, when she has finished her job, it is essential that she is given the opportunity to be clean. While this is being done by one of the family or a friend, very quickly clean her bed and put down fresh paper. At the same time you can count your new chickens and note what you have got in dogs and bitches. Before she returns to her box, she should have a quick wash down with warm water. She will feel better for this and she should go back to her new family and tuck them all in around her. There is nothing nicer than to see a happy mother with a new litter all contentedly tucking into her milk bar.

Beagle bitches usually make very good mothers. They love their families and look after them so very well. They also love all the extra care and attention and, of course, the extra food. Once again cold fresh water must be available to her at all times. An egg added to her milk or a spoonful of glucose on her food are both excellent supplements for the nursing mother.

For the first few days she will be a bit unwilling to leave her babies but she must be taken out so that she can have a walk around and make herself comfortable. Some slight discharge from the vagina may occur after whelping but this is perfectly normal, unless it goes on for more than a week when veterinary advice should be sought. If at any time a distasteful smell comes from the vagina, then do send for your veterinary surgeon straight away, as it may mean the presence of a dead puppy or just an afterbirth. This can soon be sorted out with an injection of pituitrin which your veterinary surgeon will administer.

If your bitch appears at all restless after she has finished whelping and does not settle down to the job of feeding her family and keeping them clean, then something is the matter and again veterinary help is required. Do not wait too long to call your vet, as the sooner matters are attended to the easier they are to clear up.

Some bitches suffer from uterine inertia. This is a complete absence of any labour pains and, in such cases, it is seldom that they get on with the job and produce the puppies themselves. Sometimes an injection of pituitrin helps them on their way but if not, I am afraid a Caesarean operation is the only answer. Beagles are not prone to this trouble and are usually very easy whelpers. If the bitch is attended to in good time and before she is completely exhausted, the operation should be quite successful and she should be able to rear her puppies herself.

Do not believe the old wives' tale that if a bitch has a Caesar she will not be able to have another litter. In fact, the next litter might easily be delivered quite normally. While talking about old wives' tales, there is also the other story that if a bitch is caught by a dog not of her own breed, and he mates her, she will never be able to have a proper Beagle litter. This is absolute nonsense and with no foundation whatsoever.

At about three days the whelps' dew claws should be removed. This is a tricky task unless you know exactly what you are doing, and you should leave it to an experienced person. I have seen many litters spoiled by amateurs who thought they had gone deep enough to get the root of the dew claw out only to find that they had hardly touched it at all and, of course, it grew back in. Puppies have been brought for me to give my opinion on and I am always horrified when I see these ugly little claws still there. At this age, if they have to be removed, it means a bigger scar because once they are cut out, even under a local anaesthetic, they require a stitch or two. Do have them done properly when the whelps are only three or four days old.

The puppies' nails should be trimmed about once a week. They grow very quickly when they are feeding from the bitch and not up on their legs. If they are not carefully trimmed and done regularly, the poor bitch's stomach becomes a mass of scratches from their efforts to fight to get at her teats. Once the puppies are up on their legs and getting about on hard surfaces, this job is not quite so necessary.

The puppies should start to be weaned when they are about three weeks of age or even younger if the bitch has a big litter and she seems to be losing condition. Serious digestive troubles can be caused through weaning too quickly and not making this a gradual enough process.

Beagles, of course, love their meat and to begin with we start them off with a little scraped meat given to them on a finger. It is amazing how quickly they find this and how they love it. For the first three days just one meal, if you can call it that, should be given and then this should be increased to two meals just

Mother with litter

giving a tiny little bit extra each time. From there they graduate to one meat meal plus a milk food meal, and this can be a terribly messy business until they get the hang of it. A small quantity of a milk food should be put in a dish and offered to each individual puppy. Individual feeding is necessary at this stage so that the whelps get the right idea of what to do. Beagles are very quick on the uptake and soon they know exactly what food is for. Of course, there will always be the greedy ones and the rather more refined ones, even in Beagles. When it comes to feeding them altogether or even in two lots, do watch out for the greedy ones and lift them away so that their slower brothers and sisters can get their fair share.

By the end of the first week of weaning the puppies should be getting two meals a day and so relieving the strain on their dam. Gradually this should be increased to two meat meals a day and one milk food meal and by the time they are six weeks of age they should be having two meals of each type.

By about seven weeks they should be weaned altogether and the dam kept away from them. She may wish to go back to them at night for a couple of times but, after this, she has really done her job well and should be taken away completely.

The puppies are now ready for their new homes, and for those who have just reared their first litter, this is rather a sad parting. There is very much pleasure in rearing a litter and you get to know all the little individuals in it and you have perhaps even christened them with pet names. Every litter is a great excitement, no matter whether it is your first or your hundredth. There is always something different to watch or to learn and one never ceases to marvel at the wonders of Mother Nature.

You have now reared your first litter and I am perfectly sure it will not be your last. I expect that you are perhaps even now planning another one.

The breed worldwide

I have been privileged to judge the breed in most parts of the world and there is a very good standard throughout.

America It is believed that General Richard Rowett of Carlinsville, Illinois, was the first importer of Beagles into the United States. These Beagles were imported from England and in conjunction with Mr. Norman Elmore he set about producing a strain that was well known for its excellent conformation and type. He started his strain in the late 1870s and very soon a great interest was taken in this game little hound. In 1888 the National Beagle Club was formed and this Club came under the jurisdiction of the American Kennel Club.

In 1886 General Rowett's Beagles contributed to the foundation of the Waldingfield pack, the oldest pack in America today.

After the General's death his Beagles were taken over by Mr. Pottinger Dorsey from Newmarket, Maryland, and Mr. Staley Doub, of Frederick, Maryland. These two gentlemen were more interested in the hunting qualities than in show stock but, unlike England, all Beagles in America, whether they are show Beagles or hunting Beagles, come under the Rules and Regulations of the American Kennel Club and are included in the American Kennel Club registration tables.

It is interesting to note that a hound called Champion Bannerman was exported to America to a Mr. A. C. Krueger of Pennsylvania from Mr. Crane's small type hounds in Dorset. (See the chapter on Breed History.) This dog was introduced to try to reduce size, as at this time American Beagles tended to be rather on the large size. Mr. Crane's Beagles were, of course, well known for their uniformity of type and size which was around 9-10in. (23-25cm.)

Around 1887 a Standard of the Breed was compiled by General Rowett, Dr. L. H. Twaddell and Mr. Elmore. Since this date there have been very few amendments to it. (See the chapter on The Breed Standard.)

In America Beagles are used in field trials where they hunt hare, snowshoe and rabbit. These trials are now very popular and have spread to most parts of the country and have done a great deal to popularise the Beagle. Beagles are also used extensively as gundogs. They are very capable in the art of finding their prey and driving it into the line of their masters' guns. Extremely versatile and most popular hounds, they have certainly made their mark in the USA.

The Peterborough Hound Show, which is so very popular in England and organised by the Master of Harriers and Beagles Association, has its equivalent in America in the Bryn Mawr Hound Show which is very well supported each year.

British Breeders have bought stock from America for our show ring and these hounds have acquitted themselves very well indeed, both in the show ring and as stud dogs. It is quite invidious to try to compare the American Beagles with our own. They both have their own virtues and, of course, their own faults. We have yet to find the perfect dog. They both have something to offer and perhaps it might be that by careful breeding of the American Beagles to our own show Beagles, and vice versa, one day we could claim to have that elusive creature – the perfect Beagle.

I recently judged the breed on two occasions in the United States and in California I was most impressed by several of the under 13in. (33cm.) hounds. I found them so right for type and, in the reduction in size, they had lost nothing and were absolute miniatures of the bigger hounds. I loved them dearly.

Australia Like many other breeds in Australia the rise in popularity of the Beagle has only been in the last ten or twelve years. Some of the first imports into Southern Australia came from the English kennels of Mr. and Mrs. Appleton and Mrs. Clayton and quickly won their titles. I visited Australia for the first time in 1968 and judged a very representative entry at the Pal International Dog Show. There were fifty dogs entered but today the breed can expect many more entries, and I understand the quality and standard is very level.

Lemon and white Beagles, or for that matter any other colour than tricolour, are not as popular in Australia as they are in this country. Personally I feel that the lemon/white hound gives quality in a pedigree and I would hate to be without their presence in a family tree plus the very many virtues that they pass on.

Canada Canada is very closely associated with the United States in the breeding of Beagles.

Ceylon When I last judged in Ceylon in 1968 the classes for

Beagles were divided into 14in. (35cm.) and under, and 14-16in. (35-41cm.) This little island finds very great difficulty in importing fresh stock and without it they are very much curtailed in their breeding programme. Mr. Pieris has been one of the pioneers of the Beagle in Ceylon. He purchased several from Britain in the 1950s and these came mostly from the pack hounds. Mr. Arnolda was another staunch supporter of the Beagle and had the honour of going Best in Show in Ceylon at three consecutive shows of the Ceylon Kennel Club. His dog Ceylon Champion Rozavel Colorado of Bushyield was purchased from Mrs. Thelma Gray of the UK.

Denmark In 1963 the first Beagle came to Denmark from Sweden. In 1969 I had the honour of judging the Internodisk Beagle and Basset Skue's first Championship Show. Now there are many very enthusiastic owners in this country and a great many of the Danish hounds go back to English stock.

Finland The Finnish Beagle Club was established in 1961 and in that year the first Field Trial was held. Beagles have now become very popular in this country and they have produced a very good type from some excellent hounds imported from the UK. Before a Beagle can become a full Champion in Finland it must qualify in the field.

Holland There are now many very enthusiastic breeders in this country and once again stock has been imported from Britain. The Beagle is gaining in popularity and the exhibitors are most keen to improve their stock.

Italy The breed has certainly made great strides and Prov. Paola Dondina was one of the first to import fresh bloodlines. This was about 1966 and he has built up a very strong kennel with the introduction of British stock. Prov. Dondina judges Beagles at Championship Show level in Britain.

New Zealand Some of the original Beagles in this country were owned by Mr. Lucas-Lucas during the 1939-45 war. These were later owned by Mr. Kettle who bred Bulldogs. Mrs. Molly Grocott, Mrs. Pateshall-Jones, Messrs. Giles and Ellis were among the first importers of stock from Britain and this was the basis of the New Zealand hounds plus a couple of bitches that my own kennel sent out. These two bitches were both sent out in whelp and it was a great worry to us all until they arrived safely. This they both did and whelped seven and eight puppies respectively.

A Beagle Club has recently been formed in New Zealand and the Beagle has certainly gone from strength to strength in this country.

Rhodesia Mrs. MacDonald Lucas has been carrying the flag in Rhodesia and has imported stock very successfully. There is a great deal of interest in the Beagle in this country.

Singapore Last time I judged in Singapore I had only nine Beagles shown under me. Unfortunately, there is no Breed Club to help but all the owners are most enthusiastic and the Beagle has certainly adapted itself to the conditions in Singapore.

South Africa Hare is hunted by the Beagle in South Africa and there is a pack in the country belonging to Lady Mary Grosvenor who has the Westminster Beagles. These were started in 1934 with a draft from the Cheshire Beagles. Hounds are followed on horseback and, from what I have seen of this country, this can only mean a very delightful day's outing. Many hounds have been exported from Britain and the Beagle's popularity has been steady. Mr. John Ellis of Johannesburg imported from Britain thirteen Beagles over a period of ten years and he had great success with them in the show ring. Beagles are scheduled at a great many of the shows, although it may mean travelling thousands of miles to exhibit.

South America The breed was started by Mrs. Hilda Rumboll with two imports from Britain and very many more have since followed to various parts of South America. Two English Champions have been sent to the Argentine plus other top class stock to Venezuela and Brazil. The exhibitors in South America are very keen and want to buy and exhibit only the best available. I look forward to judging them in the not too distant future.

Sweden Last but by no means least Sweden has made great progress in the breed. Mrs. Judy de Casembroot of Treetops Cocker fame exported, about fifteen years ago, Treetops Hold Fast to Mrs. Carin Lindhe of Stockholm. This bitch was a great character. Since then many good hounds have left English shores to take up residence in Sweden. The Swedish people are very shrewd and careful breeders and today they have many fine specimens of the breed. They come in good numbers to their Championship Shows.

Apart from the many other qualities of our Beagles, I do know that their memory serves them well. On many occasions, on visiting overseas countries, I have caught up with Beagles exported from our own kennels. If they have been show dogs that I have handled through their show career, they never fail to welcome me to their adopted land. They may take just a minute or two to recognise their old 'mum' but once it registers with them they are delighted to renew their friendship. This, in itself, is a charming trait and yet another of the Beagle's many virtues.

Health and first-aid

The Beagle is a very healthy, strong little dog and, provided he is given reasonable care and attention, you should have few worries in respect of his health.

Follow your diet sheet, give him sensible exercise, house him in a comfortable, draught-free bed, and he should reward you with a clean bill of health.

If you are ever worried about the health of your Beagle, never hesitate to call your veterinary surgeon. If you are choosing your veterinary surgeon for the first time, it is advisable to have one who specialises in small animals as, being a specialist in this field, he or she will be more appreciative of your dog's needs.

Abrasions Being a very active dog, the Beagle can hardly expect to lead its whole lifetime without getting a few scars or skin injuries. Clean the wound thoroughly and dry with cotton wool, thereafter annointing with zinc or calamine ointment. Bandages may be required to prevent licking but I always find that the attraction of the bandage is too much for a Beagle and that it is hardly on before it is off. If the wound has to be bandaged, then it is wise to attach to a leather collar a plastic bucket that has had the bottom taken out of it. This is done by making holes in the bottom of the bucket and threading it on to the collar with string. With its head in the bucket, the dog cannot get to its wound and, although this may look rather uncomfortable, it does allow the wound to heal quickly. I feel that this a better method than muzzling the dog, for it is then apt to rub the muzzle on the sore place.

At all times serious cuts or wounds should be dealt with as soon as possible by a veterinary surgeon.

Anal glands These glands can cause the dog great discomfort and irritation. The symptoms that indicate everything is not quite right are easily recognisable. The dog will pull its bottom along the ground as though trying to scratch it to remove the irritation. It will constantly want to lick the anus and keep looking round at it. It will even carry its tail down covering its anus as though something was jagging it. Do take the dog to your veterinary surgeon so that he can squeeze the glands and evacuate the contents. If this is done at the first sign of any symptoms, and before abscesses appear, the problem can be cleared quickly. Fortunately Beagles are not really prone to this condition.

Arthritis This is the inflammation of a joint or a disease involving a joint. Usually this is confined to our older hounds when one finds that a joint is swollen and seems painful to the dog. In bad cases the dog very often refuses to put its foot to the ground. Rest and warmth are essential and soothing remedies should be applied.

Bites If your dog is bitten by another animal, cleanse the wound and apply penicillin ointment or tincture of iodine until all the discharge stops. Thereafter a healing ointment should be applied.

Burns and scalds Unless these are of a minor nature they should not be treated at home, as there is always the question of shock no matter how slight the accident. Clean the burn and remove any foreign material such as dirt, straw, hair, food, etc. Exclude all air by applying a dressing soaked in a strong solution of tea. Most households now carry in their kitchen lotions to apply in the case of a first degree burn to a human, and the same lotions can be applied to dogs when the burn is a simple one.

Colic This is a pain in the abdomen and is generally caused by indigestion, flatulence or constipation. The pain does not usually linger but it frightens the dog and makes it restless. It may even whine or cry out. Relief is usually obtained by getting the bowels evacuated. If the pain persists, a veterinary surgeon must be consulted.

Constipation The cause of the trouble is usually a badly balanced diet. The hound finds it difficult to pass its stools which will be very hard and dry. A change of diet should be tried and another important point is that your Beagle should be having enough exercise. As I have said repeatedly throughout this book, fresh water should always be available. If a change of diet does not ease this problem, then a laxative should be given. Liquid paraffin, Milk of Magnesia or Epsom Salts in small doses over a period of time will usually be effective.

Dandruff A scurfy condition of the skin and hair. A good grooming once or twice daily with a stiff brush or hound glove will increase the circulation to the skin, stimulate its nerve supply and generally improve its condition. A lanolin or coconut oil can be rubbed into the skin and the surplus wiped off. I always feel that the feeding of a dog shows in its coat and, if it has a scurfy coat, then the feeding is not correct. Alter the diet and once again ensure that the dog has adequate exercise. A Beagle's coat should shine with good health and it is unusual to see one with a jacket that is full of dandruff.

Diarrhoea In puppies this is usually the result of worms but can easily be caused by a change in the diet and improper feeding. If worms are suspected, it is important to ascertain whether these are of the round or tape variety, as they require different remedies. There are many perfectly safe preparations on the market that can be used to eradicate these pests.

Distemper This is a highly contagious disease and no owner should fail to have his dog given the preventive inoculations. The dog will have a high temperature and will appear completely out of sorts. A discharge from the nose will appear and often a cough. Loss of appetite and general listlessness follow and the hound will have a discharge from its eyes which will appear weak and sensitive to light. The breath will be offensive and diarrhoea may or may not occur. To nurse distemper successfully is a long and patient business and there are often very nasty side effects. Do take the safer path of having your Beagle inoculated.

Ears The term 'canker' is one that is used far too loosely by the layman for anything that seems to affect the ear. Bad ears are usually neglected ears, as ulceration does not happen just overnight. If you see your hound scratching its ear, do look inside for the real trouble. Never poke into the ear with any sort of instrument. Take your dog to your veterinary surgeon for the correct treatment and then carry it out as advised by him.

External haemorrhage In the case of an accident, excessive bleeding can be controlled by bandaging dry cotton wool firmly over the injury. If this is not successful, a tourniquet may be required until professional aid can be obtained. A handkerchief, stocking or something similar should be tied tightly around the part above the injury and then tightened by putting a stick or pencil through and twisting until the flow of blood lessens. Tourniquets must be removed every ten minutes.

Eyes Beagles sometimes suffer from running eyes. This is not common but your veterinary surgeon will prescribe an ointment. If the eyes at any time seem to be dirty and filled with mucus, then it is wise to take your Beagle to your veterinary surgeon, as this could be a symptom of a much more serious problem such as a virus infection.

Feet Split pads and eczema cause the dog to nibble at its feet and this often causes lameness. Gentian violet should be applied liberally and it will take time for the sores to heal. Cysts between the toes can be a perfect nuisance and do require veterinary treatment. Inflamed claws can be caused by the hound catching its nail on wire or on some other article. These can be very sore indeed and make it very lame. Soak the paw in a hot antiseptic solution as often as possible and try and keep it clean. Any lameness should be investigated immediately.

Fits These can be caused by many things which are often associated with virus diseases. Professional advice must be sought so that an early treatment can be started.

Fleas Dogs should be checked regularly for these parasites. If not attended to, fleas and lice can be responsible for skin troubles and general disability. Dusting powders can help eradicate these pests.

Hardpad disease Canine encephalitis is caused by a virus and in many respects is very similar to distemper, but it can and does attack the central nervous system. Those animals that survive this scourge finish with a thickening and hardening of the skin on the pads and sometimes of the nose, hence the name 'hardpad'. The symptoms are similar to those of distemper and the same advice is given that the Beagle should be inoculated against this disease. Prevention is much better than the cure.

Hiccough This is not a serious complaint but it is very distressing to the dog while it lasts. It is most common in puppies and is the result of indigestion or the irritation caused by worms. To relieve the hiccoughing some bicarbonate of soda in milk usually does the trick.

Poisoning Great speed must be employed to expel any poison swallowed by a dog. Simple emetics are the best, e.g. washing soda or salt and water. If the dog has been stung by a bee the sting should be extracted if possible. The spot should then be treated with TCP or carbonate of soda. If the dog is stung by a wasp, the wound should be treated with vinegar or acid, and in both cases it is advisable to have the animal injected with anti-histamine for a quick result.

Shock This can occur after severe injury or after anything which strongly affects the nervous system. The dog must be kept as quiet as possible and warm. A dog that is not fully conscious should never be persuaded to swallow any liquid. If it is able to swallow naturally and without choking, then a drop of brandy or whisky in water can be very helpful.

Skin conditions To the layman all skin troubles are labelled 'mange' without a proper diagnosis. The only way to make a reliable diagnosis is for a veterinary surgeon to take a skin scraping.
Sarcoptic mange This is caused by a little parasite and is contagious and very easily communicated by means of bedding, brushes, kennels, etc. It usually attacks the skin around the eyes, the outside of the ears, the elbows and on the abdomen. Small red spots, like flea bites, appear and the acrid matter that they excrete sets up intense irritation causing the dog to scratch and bite itself, thus creating nasty sore places and bare patches. It is readily cured with modern drugs such as tetmosol and benzyl benzoate.
Follicular mange This type of mange usually starts off with a single bare patch that is a dirty greyish colour. Unlike sarcoptic there is little or no irritation present although it is a parasitic condition. Under a microscope the parasite looks like a small maggot. Some believe that this skin disease is congenital and is passed on from family to family and that it is not contagious. It is far more difficult to cure than sarcoptic and veterinary help must be sought.

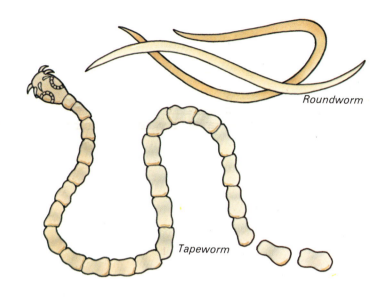
Roundworm

Tapeworm

Adult flea

Biting louse

Engorged female tick

Mite (microscopic)

Sucking louse

Parasites

Eczema This is a non-contagious skin disease and it is thought to be mainly dietary in cause. The skin is irritable and the dog scratches continually and licks itself. This continual nibbling does not help at all. It makes the parts sore and red and helps the disease to spread, and, from then on, it becomes rather sticky with a discharge. Cut hair away from the sticky part and apply benzyl benzoate or an ointment which has been found to be effective. Most kennel owners have their own special preparation for wet eczema but the above two are generally used. The dog may have to wear a hood to stop him getting at the sore parts.

Skin troubles, without an experienced eye, are not easy to diagnose and one should never jump to conclusions before a full report made by a veterinary surgeon has been received. Some forms of dermatitis and other skin eruptions caused by an allergy can look like mange. The only way to avoid these skin problems is to make sure that the dog is given regular grooming, a correct diet and proper exercise.

Snake bites Very few snake bites in Britain are serious. Adders do spring up now and again and if your dog is bitten by an adder take action immediately. A bandage should be applied as tightly as possible above the part bitten and between the bite and the heart. This prevents the poison spreading into the bloodstream. Open up the bite and push into it crystals of permanganate of potash and call your veterinary surgeon. Keep your dog as comfortable as possible, and here again a little drop of brandy will not hurt.

Sunstroke or heatstroke Always see that your dog has a good supply of water in his run and, if he has to be left out in his run for any length of time, he must have adequate shade. In a hot summer sunstroke is not at all unusual. The signs are excessive panting with profuse salivation, followed by weakness of the limbs, almost a staggering gait, and then complete collapse. Put the dog into a cool place at once and apply ice and cold water to his head, neck and shoulders. I once saved a very well known dog by simply plunging him into a tank of cold water with just his head above the surface. Keep him there for just a few minutes and then remove him to a quiet cool area and give him a drink. It is quite amazing how quickly the dog will come round if you catch him in time.

Beagling

*'I like the hunting of the hare;
New sports I hold in scorn,
I like to be as my fathers were
In the days ere I was born'*
WILFRID BLUNT

I never feel that a book on Beagles is complete without a little mention of the art and the fun of beagling. After all, each and every one of our Beagles came originally from stock that hunted and it would be wrong of us to try to pretend that this was not so — even if we wanted to. All through the ages this great sport has existed and given tremendous pleasure, excitement and relaxation to everyone associated with it. In the early days horses were used, but nowadays this is frowned upon and most packs forbid anyone to come out on horseback.

Beagling is the art of hunting hare with Beagles which rely completely on their noses to work out the tricky and devious path that she has taken. The hare is a very wily animal and is well capable of deceiving the Beagles by her many tricks. She is highly intelligent and she has been known on occasions to jump on to the top of a wall and hide until the hounds have passed. Water also gives her defence against her many enemies, and well she knows this. By taking a quick dip and crossing and recrossing a stream she decreases her scent and this permits her to rest a while and take stock of her position and work out her next move. She is not averse to getting mixed up with the cattle and sheep and rolling in their excreta to disguise her scent. Her intelligence and instinct should never be underrated. She is as agile as the finest athlete and she has her own particular beauty. She is called the common brown hare, but there is so much quality about her that she should never be described as common. She is essentially a creature of the wild and one who fights a lone battle, so often very successfully.

Beagling is one of the most inexpensive of all sports as, apart from requiring a very comfortable pair of shoes (tennis shoes or running shoes are ideal), plus some warm clothing if the weather demands it, there is no further equipment required. Hounds do not live on air, of course, and they require someone to look after them. To help with this expense those

A brace of Beagles showing the use of a brace lead

who are not actually members of the Hunt are asked to contribute to the 'cap'. This is a very small thank you for an exhilarating and exciting day in the country in good company.

I think one could safely say that beagling is the only sport where the participants can please themselves as to how much exercise they want to take. Grandfather can happily accompany grandson and both can enjoy themselves to the full, the youngster keeping up with the hounds and the older man viewing from a hill top and transporting himself in his car when the hounds move on. No one worries if you wish to amble along catching a glimpse of the pack now and then while listening to the tales of the old hands. If you lose the pack, there will always be someone well able and willing to tell you in which direction they have gone. The only thing that you simply must not do is carelessly and thoughtlessly to cross the line of the hare and spoil the scent. There would be loud screams from the huntsmen and unwelcome glares and mumbles from the followers.

It is not only a sport for the young but also for the young of heart, whose spirit is still willing although the flesh and limb may be a little weak. Beaglers, like the Beagles, are a happy band of people who come out for the purpose of enjoying themselves, be it icy cold, wet and shivery or a glorious crisp November morning. It is seldom, if ever, under reasonable hunting conditions, that the hounds disappoint in their task.

I would like to quote from Miss Augusta G. Guest who wrote in 1910 as follows:

'I think the beauty of our modern Beagle is that he hunts himself, and for himself and his pack; he is not jealous, and his musical little voice proclaims to all when he has picked up the line. A hare carries an indifferent scent – I believe all Harrier and Beagle men will agree to that – far different from the little red rover who leaves a record of his whereabouts to more noses than one.'

Many and varied are the theories with regard to the scent of hunted creatures. It is thought that, as far as the hare is concerned, her scent comes from the glands between the toes of her pads. The weight of her body, as she scampers over the ground, imprints it on the ground and it then proceeds to evaporate and to spread. How quickly it spreads and how strong the scent is depends entirely on the prevailing weather conditions. This can vary from day to day, even from hour to hour. A really good day's hunting depends entirely on a good scent and it is such an imponderable thing. I feel that maybe Mr. Jorrocks had it nearly right when he said: 'Constant only in its inconstancy – there is nothing so queer as scent, 'cept a woman.'

The Beagles have no easy task but, if they are skilfully directed by their Master or Huntsman, they will give a very capable and determined account of themselves displaying excellent hound work that is second to none. Many famous Masters of Foxhounds have learned their first lesson on how to hunt with the Beagles. The capability of the Master or Huntsman to display the great talents of his pack is of the utmost importance and can make or mar a day's hunting, just as the weather can. Mr. Jorrocks said of huntsmen that they are 'either 'eaven born or hidiots'.

The pack should always be as consistent in size as possible so that the speed is as uniform as possible. The old Mexican proverb says 'one fast mule in a team of slow ones makes no end of distress for its Master, its mates and itself'. This applies to any hunting pack, be it Beagles, Foxhounds, Harriers or Otterhounds. Any hounds with serious faults, such as rioting, babbling, running mute or skirting, should not be included in the pack and, as no other pack can reasonably be expected to welcome them, they should not be drafted to another pack. One naughty hound can upset the whole pack and there is nothing more annoying to the Master, Huntsman or the followers, than to have a rebel of some sort that disrupts, or tries to disrupt, the whole of the day's sport. There is no prettier sight than to witness a well matched, well disciplined, pack of Beagles hunting their hare, sorting out her scent, keeping up with her turning and twisting, with not a single straggler or dissenter to spoil the picture.

Details of the various meets are usually given in the local paper. If not, pop into the local pub and there they will know all the details that you require. Get to the Meet in good time and remember to keep well behind the Master when he moves off. Watch what the old hands do and you will soon learn the tricks of the trade. Provided you obey the rules of the hunting world, you will be most welcome and you will have found for yourself a new recreation and new friends.

A quick sharp note on the horn from the Master tells everyone that the quarry has been sighted. You might just catch a glimpse of her over the hedge. The Beagles have their noses down and they are off. They are so thrilled and they throw out such happy music with sweet melodious tones. You find yourself driven forward by the urge to be with them and you keep up with the field. Don't get too excited — keep well behind the hounds and save what energy you can. It is a long day and it may be that the hare will turn in her ways and come right back the way she has been. Save yourself a journey if you can. As already said, watch what the old hands are doing — it is more than likely that they will have a good idea as to the path of the hare. Isn't this just the right sort of tonic for those who are shut up in stuffy offices or factories throughout the week? Here in the good country air one can let off steam in excellent company. Your feet may get soaked, your legs may be very weary indeed and your mouth may be dry but I am perfectly certain that, once having known the joy and freedom of such an afternoon, you will be determined to take part as often as possible in this sport of kings.

It is not the end when the day's hunting is finished. You have yet to sample a good Beagle tea. This is usually provided by some very kind farmer's wife and as all the home baking is consumed the inquest on the day's proceedings takes place. It is all part and parcel of a day's beagling; the companionship, the fresh air, the exercise, the excitement, the hare and the hounds.

Just before you say farewell to your new-found friends, make sure that you remembered to pay your 'cap', and that you remembered to say 'thank you' to the Master for your initiation to this sport and for a wonderful day. You did, of course, shut any gates that you opened. If not, it is unpardonable, and the farmer whose land you have been over will hardly welcome you back.

Many of our Beagle Clubs, which come under the Rules of the Kennel Club, have working sections that organise Drag Hunts. Working Certificates are awarded to the hounds who, in the opinion of the judges, hunt well enough to qualify. They require that a hound should hunt the same line of drag without changing for not less than ten minutes for novices, fifteen minutes for intermediates and twenty minutes for senior hounds. These Meets are organised privately by the Clubs, usually on a Sunday, and they give marvellous sport to the supporters who turn out to see the show hounds at work.

The drag is a trail made by dragging or pulling a 'scent' over a chosen bit of country. This is done either by a runner on foot or someone on horseback. The scent can be a piece of rag or cloth with aniseed oil dabbed on it, or a fairly fresh dead hare, or even the droppings of a fox. The lines should be rather short for the beginners and gradually longer and more involved for more experienced hounds. This is terrific fun for both owners and their show hounds, and I do not know who enjoys the day's outing most. I have attended several most successful afternoons even though the scent has only been aniseed. Yet another example of how truly versatile our Beagle can be.

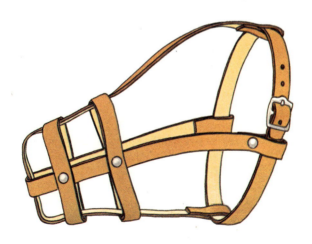

A suitable muzzle for the Beagle, when required or advised

USEFUL ADDRESSES

The Kennel Club, 1 Clarges Street, Piccadilly, London W1Y 8AB, England.

The American Kennel Club, 51 Madison Avenue, New York, N.Y. 10010, U.S.A.

There are many clubs catering for this breed and the addresses of these can be obtained from your Kennel Club.

DOG MAGAZINES

Pure Bred Dogs, the American Kennel Gazette, published by the American Kennel Club.

Dog World, 22 New Street, Ashford, Kent, England.

Our Dogs, 5 Oxford Road Station Approach, Manchester 1, England.

READING LIST

Appleton and Appleton. *Beagles and Beagling.* Kaye and W., 1970.

Gordon, John F. *Beagle Guide.* The Pet Library Inc., 1968.

Gray, Thelma. *The Beagle.* Popular Dogs Publishing Co. Ltd., 1970.

Harmar, Hilary. *Dogs and How to Breed Them.* John Gifford Ltd., 1974.

Lyon, McDowell. *The Dog in Action.* Howell Book House, 1966.

Index